ABIDE IN LOVE

ABIDE IN LOVE

ERNESTO CARDENAL

Foreword by
THOMAS MERTON

Photographs by
MEV PULEO

ORBIS BOOKS

Maryknoll, New York 10545

The Catholic Foreign Mission Society of America (Maryknoll) recruits and trains people for overseas mission-ary service. Through Orbis Books, Maryknoll aims to foster the international dialogue that is essential to mission. The books published, however, reflect the opinions of their authors and are not meant to represent the official position of the society.

Published by Orbis Books, Maryknoll, NY 10545–0308

Manufactured in the United States of America

Library of Congress Cataloging-in-Publication Data is available from the Library of Congress, Washington, D.C.

ISBN 1-57075-011-4

CONTENTS

FOREWORD
by Thomas Merton

I N A TIME of conflict, anxiety, war, cruelty, and confusion, the reader may be surprised that this book is a
hymn in praise of love, telling us that "all beings love
one another."

Perhaps we are too much used to saying that one *ought*
to love (thereby giving to understand that, generally
speaking, we do not love). We know that there is a *duty*
to love, that we have received a *commandment* to love
each other. But we take it for granted that we hardly ever
obey this commandment. And thus we conclude that the
world is evil because there is so little love in it, and we
blame and castigate those whom we hold responsible for
this lack of love.

Thus a theology or ethics of punishment and retri-
bution takes the place of the vision of love, and love
becomes an idealized abstraction. The daily reality of

our lives is not under the rule of love, but under the rule of law, of force, and of punishment. We talk about love, but we live by hate: we hate in the name of love. In this situation it becomes necessary to assert once more that to love is *not* impossible. Love is not something unreal. On the contrary, love is the *only* reality. Everything that is, is by virtue of love, and if love is not clearly evident in all things, the reason is that we ourselves have made no effort to *see* love in all things. In a very radical sense, love is the only and unique possibility. And everything that is not love is essentially and basically impossible.

The purpose of this book is quite simply to open our eyes to what ought to be obvious but sounds incredible: that "all beings love one another," that "all life is love." This book therefore does not say that we ought to love, nor does it lament the fact that actually we do not love. It does not tell us in great detail how we should be punished for our failure to love. It simply tells us that all things love one another, and it adds that, as a matter of fact, we do love, whether we know it or not. It asserts that we can never cease loving. Even the atheist loves God without knowing it. If we live in discord with each other and with God, it is not because we do not love, but because we do not understand and accept the fact that we are bound to love of necessity.

Psychoanalysis has taught us that much hate and fear, and even many physical illnesses, are caused by a love that refuses to acknowledge itself as such, a love that has become ill because it fails to recognize its true nature and has lost sight of its object. The conflicts that beset our world are not caused by the absence of love, but by a love that no longer recognizes itself, a love that has become disloyal to its own reality. Cruelty is misdirected love, and hate is frustrated love.

The lucid and "Franciscan" simplicity of Father Cardenal shows us the world not as we see it, with fear and distrust in our hearts, but as it is in reality. Love is not a dream. It is the basic law of all those creatures who were created free in order to give themselves to others, free to partake of the infinite abundance of life with which God has filled our being. Love is the heart and the true center of that creative dynamism that we call life. Love is life itself in its state of maturity and perfection.

The saints were capable of seeing through the masks

that cover the faces of humanity, and they saw that the masks are unreal. In the innumerable faces of human beings they saw only one face: the face of love (that is to say, the face of Christ). This is what Ernesto Cardenal has seen and written down. His entire book is an ever repeated discovery, an ever new poetic intuition of the central reality of life. It is a hymn to life, and this is why it is so eminently truthful. With depth of conviction Cardenal speaks again and again of that which simply *is. Love is.* All else *is not.* All that is has its being and its action in love.

Non-rational creatures are guided by a love that they do not know, toward an end that they do not understand. For the animal lives in nature without being conscious of it and without that freedom that is the gift of conscious existence. The animal lives immersed in life, a life without reflection. We might therefore say that the animal is "animated" by life and by love in a passive manner and without being cognizant of it. The animal has no other choice than this "being animated" by its own nature.

This, as Rainer Maria Rilke said in the *Duino Elegies,* is

the reason why the animal is always in immediate contact with life. Consciousness never intervenes between the animal and life. The animal never reflects on life but simply *lives,* and living is its only way of knowing. The animal does not recognize itself as being alive; it simply lives what it cognizes.

The gift of consciousness is a divine blessing, but it may turn into a curse if we do not want it to be a blessing. If consciousness, as Rilke saw it, were a pure consciousness of love, our love would be as immediate and spontaneous as life itself. As the animal is "animated" immediately and directly by the life of nature, we would be activated and motivated in the inwardness of our consciousness by supernatural and divine love. Our consciousness would then not be dimmed by a feeling of frustration on account of our limitations. It would be a pure consciousness of love, of God, and of life as a gift of love.

As human persons, however, we are not merely "animated" or "vitalized" by our nature. We are autonomous, conscious of ourselves, capable of betraying our nature (even though incapable of changing it) and thus capable of either affirming or denying our nature. We are capable of being or becoming human, whether we like it or not. We are capable of being children of God with the full consent of our will or contrary to our will. We can accept ourselves or reject ourselves. We are capable of loving others freely, spontaneously, with complete overtness, or we may prefer to reject and despise them, and in this case we will still love them, even though contrary to their own will. We will love them unknowingly. Thus, even though we still love, our love has turned against our own self. It has become adulterated, contaminated, and disingenuous. That love with which, in the depth of our heart, we want to open ourselves to others, turns in upon us and is locked up inside us. The love that could and should give nourishment to others consumes itself. The love that should have found its full realization in self-giving founders in the confusion and the torment of negation. And it is ironic that negation often hides under the name of love.

Creation in its totality could teach us how to love if only we were willing to accept its teaching. Life as such is love, and if it is lived in truth, it teaches us to love.

But when human consciousness has been corrupted by the rejection of love, human beings, who are God's creatures, remake the world in their own image, and the result is a world filled with cruelty, greed, hate, fear, and strife. If, on the other hand, we consent to love and give ourselves over to life in its pristine purity — life as a pure gift of God — the entire world is overflowing with love.

Isaac of Stella, a Cistercian mystic of the twelfth century, writes:

This visible world serves man, its master, in two ways: it nourishes him and it teaches him. As a good servant, the world nourishes and teaches, provided that man be not a bad master. A bad master is stupid and wretched; his eyes may be able to penetrate with their glance to the ends of the world and yet see nothing but darkness, and he will then make the world subservient to his body and his stomach. He has no longer any idea why the world was created. He believes that this immense universe was made by God for the sake of his small belly.

Isaac of Stella was surely aware of the meaning and importance of nourishment, and he was familiar with the joys of festive meals. God is given to us in the eucharistic meal, so that man might be capable of communion with God in the gifts of the earth and the fruits of our labor. Isaac knows of the pleasures of wine and of festivity, but he is aware that these are only images of the sublime joy of that love by which God gives to us the divine spirit like a "torrent of delight that inebriates us with a fervor of charity." Love is for Isaac that divine wine that intoxicates and enraptures us. God wants us to drink of this wine, but we are afraid to do so, notwithstanding God's continuous invitation.

This book is filled with invitations to drink and to delight in the banquet of love. Or, to say it much better, it invites us to open our eyes and look at the world around us so that we may recognize that the festive meal is right in front of us, that the wine, unbeknown to us, is within the reach of our hand.

These basic principles illuminate for us both the creative dynamism of nature and the refreshing and redeeming dynamism of grace. However, these simple principles cannot be acquired in the splendid tepidity of abstract meditation. These pages are filled with the concrete firmness of conviction because the author wrote them after having completely surrendered to love when he entered a strictly contemplative monastic community far away from his homeland. Love has its seat not only in the mind or in the heart; it is more than mere thought and desire. Love is action, and it is only in the action of love that we attain to the contemplative intuition of loving wisdom. This contemplative intuition is an act of the highest degree and kind; it is the purest kind of love. And this love does away with the apparent contradiction between action and contemplation.

In order to attain to such a mature act of love, we must first have experienced contradiction and conflict. Love is the pinnacle of freedom and of a fully personalized consciousness. And love discovers its own being only in the act of love. A love that acts without being fully conscious of its action acts contrary to its very nature and does not attain to a full consciousness of self. It remains, as it were, in hiding before itself. Nor is it capable of acting perfectly in accordance with its own nature.

Those who act remain then somehow separated from their love, and their action does not measure up to the fullness of their love. Love here is in contradiction with itself. It rules the heart with a strange and oppressive passion. It carries with it bitterness, anxiety, repression, violence, and even a taste of death. For every love that is not a totally free and spontaneous self-giving harbors a taste of death. This means then that all our love — the love of us average human beings, who are neither saints nor mystics — is beset with contradiction, conflict, and bitterness. And it carries with it a taste of death.

What shall we say of this kind of love? That it should not be? That it is sinful? That it should not be permitted or should be punished? Alas, it is surely true that our poor love tastes of sin. However, Ernesto Cardenal says of it simply that it is *love,* but a love that is not yet sufficiently free, not yet sufficiently pure. And we might add that by what it lacks in being true love we may discover the way that leads to true and perfect love. It is by *accepting this imperfect love, fully conscious of its imperfection, that our love may be made perfect.*

The first step on the way to true and perfect love is

the admission that our love, even though not yet pure, is nonetheless love and that by virtue of its very nature it aspires to become pure.

Our moralists sometimes tell us that what is needed is justice, righteousness, honesty, truth, and love; that there should be no room for egotism, iniquity, and injustice; that egotism should be eradicated and love should be made obligatory.

For the moralist human life is a complex system of virtues and vices, and love is assigned a definite place in the system; it is one of the several virtues. However the mystics know of no such complex system; for them love is the one and the all. For them the virtues are different aspects of love, and they hold that the same is true of the vices. The virtues are manifestations of a love that is alive and hale. And the vices are symptoms of an enfeebled love, of a love that refuses to be what it is in its essence.

Actually there is nothing else but love. But this love may live in contradiction with itself. It may at one and the same time be love and hate, love and greed, love and fear, love and envy, love and lust. It is destined, however, to be simply love, without any self-contradictory admixture. And love cannot fulfill its true destiny if we merely try to suppress our hatreds, our greeds, our fears, our jealousies, our lusts. These evil forces receive their strength solely from love. To suppress them is to suppress love. On the contrary, these evil drives ought to be made fully conscious of themselves as love in disguise, and if this is the case, they will not be able to divert the potency of love to the service of that which is not love.

This means that the root of evil and of moral infirmity is ignorance with regard to the kind of love that fails to recognize its true identity and that is therefore blind with respect to its true being and its strength. In the measure in which love begins to become conscious of itself, it recognizes its self-betrayal. It is confused by the spectacle of its radical inner discord. It is frightened by the sight of its divided self and thus becomes the prey of great anguish. For this reason a feeble love prefers to remain unconscious of itself or to know itself only in the form of some disguise. In the degree to which it becomes conscious of itself, it becomes conscious of its inherent contradictions. And thus all our conventional love, if we dare face it, recognizes itself as impure, anguished, divided, and burdened with suffering. Such a love is therefore a veritable agony in the original sense of this term — a tremendous *struggle*. Although God wanted life to be a pure consciousness of love and peace, it is actually a fierce struggle, because in our actual human existence life is the agony of a love that fears to accept itself, aware of the fact that it is self-contradictory — self-affirmation and self-negation at one and the same time. "Those who live in constant struggle live in agony, fighting against life itself," wrote Unamuno.

This, then, is the central problem of every human love. Regardless of how pure love may be, our love is divided by an inherent self-contradiction as long as we are weak human beings, living on this earth and in time. Our love repulses and negates itself. Only God's love is perfectly pure. And human love can only approximate that divine purity in the mystic or the saint who is wholly filled with the love of God. All others (including the one who may some day become a mystic but is not one yet) are bound to live in the anguish of contradiction, or perhaps to be content with a love that is not fully conscious of itself. We experience in ourselves the anguish of this inner conflict from the moment we begin to love. To accept love into our conscious life is to accept simultaneously the consciousness of our agony.

The basic contradiction that love has to face is the contradiction between life and death. A false religious idealism imagines sometimes that it can choose a life without death. Actually, however, to choose life is to choose death, since the temporal life we live as human beings terminates in death. To "accept" another form of life, one in which we shall never have to face death, is to accept an illusion. An earthly life without death is a mere dream. And even the acceptance of "eternal life" means for the Christian the prior acceptance of a temporal life that ends with death. Thus death cannot be evaded. It is a part of life, and it actually imparts meaning to life because it involves a basic contradiction that is essential for an understanding of human existence. Why should Christ have died on the cross if death were simply an absurdity? Christ's death rests on the presupposition that every death is tragic. And his death imparts to every death a dimension of hope and of victory. Christ on the cross hallowed the agony of love. The gift that Christ offers to those who love is the cross, and it is this gift that purifies love.

To love life as it really is means to accept it in its total reality, which includes death, to accept not only the *idea* of death but also those acts that anticipate death in the offering and giving of ourselves.

As Unamuno told us, the materialistic definition of life as a "conjunction of functions that resist death" makes of life a struggle against truth, and "a struggle against death and thus also against truth, against the truth of death."

In a sense, every sacrifice of our personal interest and our pleasure for the sake of another person or simply for the act of "love" is a kind of death. But at the same time it is an act of life and an affirmation of the truth of life. Every time love accepts a partial "death," it reaffirms itself as life, triumphs over death, and overcomes the self-contradiction of life within us. For this reason love actually demands this intrinsic contradiction to realize itself in our lives.

The metaphysical structure of love is in a certain sense

dialectic. Love demands conflict; it nourishes itself by conflict and emerges purified from conflict. But once love attains to its authentic purity in the fire of conflict, it causes the conflict to disappear and with it disappears the contradiction. Thus, even in the midst of conflict, love is able to affirm with absolute certitude: "All things love each other; everything is love." And this is not merely an idea but rather the point of a concrete *act*. Without this act, the idea is meaningless.

Love, then, is both action and intuition. And, over and above these, it is a *presence*. It is an act by which our freely offered sacrifice transcends that contradiction of life and death that has its locus in the depth of our being. Love is an act of surrender and the intuition of a freedom beyond life and death, but of a freedom that can be attained only by self-surrender in the midst of self-contradiction. Love becomes perfect in a dialectic of action and intuition, culminating in the mysterious presence of Someone who is invisible but who *is love*. And now we understand that both the act and the intuition of love issue from this presence.

It is of such acts, such intuitions, and such presences

that these meditations were born, meditations that dare to affirm: there is nothing but love; everything is love. And all that which seems to be distinct from love and which even seems to contradict love, is in reality love. However, in order to see this, one has to love. One has to love wholly, totally, and one has to be willing to accept conflict and contradiction. One has to accept the death of love in order to be able to live the life of love. Once we accept this, we shall see that the conflict disappears and that in reality there is no contradiction, but only love.

A Master of Novices (at least this is my opinion) must above all be a person who does not meddle in affairs that are none of his business. A monastery is a *schola caritatis* — a school of love — but it is not human beings who are the teachers of love; it is the Spirit of Love that is the teacher of love. And it is the function of the human teacher to help the novices to listen to the authentic voice of the Spirit and not to allow themselves to be deceived by forms of adulterated love, no matter how spiritual they may appear to be. This is why the monastery is an ideal school of freedom, in which the monks learn to obey in the incidentals of life in order to be free in what is essential, that is, free to love. And love of God is a private personal problem for each individual. During the ten years that I was Master of Novices at Gethsemani Abbey in Kentucky, I never attempted to find out what the novices were writing down in the notebooks they kept in their desks. If they wished to talk about it, they were free to do so. Ernesto Cardenal was a novice at Gethsemani for two years, and I knew about his notes and his poems. He spoke to me about his ideas and his meditations. I also knew about his simplicity, his loyalty to his vocation, and his dedication to love. But I never imagined that some day I was going to write an introduction to the simple meditations he was writing down in those days, nor that in reading them (almost ten years later) I would find in them so much clarity, profundity, and maturity. What we meet here is more than a systematic doctrine: it is an intuitive knowledge of the profound truth of Christian life. A Christian is united with God in Christ through love. And so this book is entirely traditional; it reminds us at times of St. Augustine or of the mystics of "Bridal Union" of the German Rhineland. And yet it is also entirely modern, bearing resemblance to the vision of Teilhard de Chardin. It is also absolutely sincere in its great simplicity, a quality that is surely one of the principal signs of the authenticity of spiritual teaching.

Ernesto Cardenal left Gethsemani Abbey because of ill health. However, today I can see that this is not the only reason: it did not make sense to continue at Gethsemani as a novice and as a student when actually he was already a teacher. Today he is an ordained priest and the founder of a contemplative community that lives in the spirit of the wisdom and in the humility of love that are so signally evident in these pages. His community is located precisely at a place where it is most needed — in Central America, where there are no contemplative religious orders. The book of Father Cardenal, this hymn to life and love, gives testimony of the renewal of the church in Latin America. It is, we believe, a sign of the dawn of a new day in these countries of the future. They will not only attain temporal freedom and prosperity, but will also learn to sing hymns to life and to love, thus bringing to fruition the abundant potentialities that are still dormant and hidden in that rich, volcanic soil.

ABIDE IN LOVE

Oneness

ALL THINGS love one another. Everything in nature feels fellowship with all the rest. All living beings are in communion with each other. All plants, animals, and things have family features and copy one another. There are insects that imitate flowers and flowers that imitate insects, animals that are like water, rocks, the sand of the desert, snow, trees, or other animals. All living beings love one another (and eat one another), and they are all joined in the vast process of birth, growth, reproduction, and death. All things in nature know the process of mutation, transformation, and change, from the one into the other; they hug and caress and kiss. And like the laws governing living things, the laws governing inert nature (which also has an invisible life) are all contained in the one law of love. All physical phenomena are the one phenomenon of love. The condensation of the snowflake is one with the explosion of a new star, a nova. The beetle clinging to its dung-dropping is one with the lover clinging to his love.

All things are related; one is contained in another and that other in others still, so that the whole universe is one immense being.

Everything in nature tries to break down its own limits and transcend the confines of its individuality, seeking someone to whom to give itself, into whom to transform itself. The laws of thermodynamics and electrodynamics, the laws of light and universal gravity are all one and the same law of love. Everything in nature is incomplete as it offers itself to another and clasps that other to itself. All beings in their most secret self and inmost depth hunger and thirst for love.

All things are related; one is contained in another and that other in others still, so that the whole universe is one immense being.

The whole of nature touches and intertwines in one great embrace. The wind that brushes against my skin, the sun that kisses my face, the air that I breathe, the fish swimming in the water, the far-off star, and the gaze in which I hold it are all in contact. What we call the empty space between the stars is made of the same matter as the stars themselves, except that it is thinner and more rarefied. The stars are merely a denser concentration of this interstellar matter, and the whole universe is like one big star. We all share in this universe through one and the same rhythm, the rhythm of universal gravity, which is the force binding chaotic matter, joining molecules, bringing particles of matter together at any particular point in the universe, and causing the stars to be stars. This is the rhythm of love.

We are all in contact and we are all incomplete. And this incomplete nature strains toward its own perfection. This is called evolution. The most perfect thing in nature is humankind. We also are incomplete. We too are imperfect and strain toward another, toward God. And when we love God, we love God with the urgency of all nature, with the groaning of the creatures, and all the desire implicit in evolution. The whole of creation groans with us, as St. Paul says, as if it were in labor. It is the pain of the mighty process of evolution.

The monks in choir are singing in the name of all creation, for everything in nature — from the electron to human beings — is a single psalm. We cannot rest till we find God, who alone can satisfy our hearts, who alone can bear the enormous love that strains with all

We are all in contact and we are all incomplete.

All creation calls God, in all its many languages.

the force of universal gravity. It is toward God that all creatures strain.

And all things speak to us of God, because all things long for God, the starry sky and all minuscule insects, the huge galaxies and the busy chipmunk.

All stars move toward God, and the expansion of the universe is toward God. All stars and the primeval gas itself came from God, and only in God can the universe find rest.

Thirst

THE COYOTE HOWLING in the night calls for God and so does the hooting owl. The gentle dove coos for God and does not know it. The little calf mooing for its mother is also calling God, as is the lion who roars and the croaking frogs. All creation calls God, in all its many languages. Lovers and poets as well as monks in prayer also cry to God.

All human eyes have longing in them. People of all races, children, the old, mothers, women in love, police officers, workers, adventurers, murderers, revolutionaries, dictators, and saints all have the same light of longing, the same deep fire, the same infinite desire for happiness and joy without end. Human eyes are like wells, like the well of the Samaritan woman.

Every woman is a woman at the well. The well is deep. And Jesus is sitting on the rim of the well.

"And the woman said to him, 'Sir, you have nothing to draw with and the well is deep...'

"Jesus said to her, 'Every one who drinks of this water will thirst again, but whoever drinks of the water that I shall give him will never thirst; the water that I shall give him will become in him a spring of water welling up to eternal life.'

"The woman said to him, 'Sir, give me this water that I may not thirst.'"

This thirst felt by all beings is the love of God.

For this love's sake, all crimes are committed, all wars are fought, and all people love or hate each other. For this love's sake human beings climb mountains, go

All human eyes have longing in them.

7

God's arrow has pierced every heart.

down to the ocean bed; they rule and plot, build and write, sing and cry and love. Every human action, even sin, is a search for God. But sometimes God is sought where God cannot be found. Thus St. Augustine: "Seek what you seek but not where you seek it." For what we seek in orgies, at parties, on journeys, in movie theaters and bars is simply God, who is all the time only to be found within ourselves.

Within every one of us there is the same cry and the same thirst. So the psalmist writes: "As the deer thirsts for running waters, so longs my soul, O God, for thee." God's arrow has pierced every heart.

The dictator's lust for power, money, and property is the love of God. The lover finding her way to the house of her beloved, the explorer, the business executive, the agitator, the artist, and the contemplative monk are all looking for the same thing: heaven.

God is everyone's homeland. For God alone we are homesick. From every creature God calls us. We hear that call deep within us, as the lark hears its mate calling at daybreak, or Juliet hears Romeo whispering beneath her balcony.

Evening and night are quiet and solitary because God made them for contemplation. Woods, deserts, the sea, and the starry sky were made for contemplation. Indeed, for this the world was made.

Magpies and fishes speak of God, and it is God who taught them their language. The bird chorus in the early morning sings to God. Volcanoes, clouds, and trees shout about God. All creation proclaims with a loud voice the existence, the beauty, and the love of God. Music sings this message in our ears, as the beautiful countryside communicates it to our eyes.

"I find letters from God dropped in the street and every one of them is signed by him," says Walt Whitman. And the green grass is a fragrant handkerchief with God's initials on the corner; as Whitman says, God dropped it on purpose to remind us of him. That is how the saints see nature, and how Adam saw it in Eden (and how poets and artists also see it, at least some of the time).

God's signature is on the whole of nature. All creatures are love letters from God to us. They are outbursts of love. The whole of nature is bursting with love, set in

God's signature is on the whole of nature. All creatures are love letters from God to us.

9

Nature is like God's shadow, reflecting God's beauty and splendor.

it by God, who is love, to kindle the fire of love in us. All things have no other reason for existing, no other meaning. They can give us no satisfaction or pleasure beyond this, to stir in us the love of God.

Nature is like God's shadow, reflecting God's beauty and splendor. The quiet blue lake has the splendor of God. God's fingerprints are upon every particle of matter. In every atom is an image of the Trinity, the figure of the triune God. That is why God's creation so fills us with enthusiasm.

And my body was also made for the love of God. Every cell in my body is a hymn to my creator and a declaration of love.

As the kingfisher was made to fish and the humming bird to suck nectar from flowers, so we were made for contemplation and the love of God.

God is everywhere, not just within us. But God is also within us, and we have felt God's presence and desired it and that is why we withdraw into silence and solitude. For the time being we want no other creature to impress us, only God. As the lake reflects the sky when it is calm, we find God's reflection best in solitude and peace. We have only to be quiet and purified for God's face to show. And God's face is the Human One, whose face was printed on Veronica's veil. And God's face can be seen, though less clearly, in all creation.

We are mirrors of God, created to reflect God. Even when the water is disturbed, it still reflects the sky.

We are mirrors of God, created to reflect God.

Voices

ALL NATURE speaks and sings with an articulate voice. All things whisper, sigh, moan, warble, whistle, bellow, howl, roar, wail, shriek, cry, or complain. The voice of the grasshopper, cricket, and frog, the chatter of chipmunks calling each other, and all animal sounds are a prayer. So is the human voice. That is why contemplative monks are silent. They have dedicated their voices to sing only in choir, because they have understood that the voice is a prayer.

All nature consists of symbols that speak to us of God.

Each one of us bears God's handwriting, and our whole being is a message from God.

Creation is in God's handwriting, in which every sign makes sense. The path of meteors in the sky and the trail of mollusks on the sand, the formations of migrating birds on autumn evenings, the sun's course through the zodiac and the circles in the trunk of the cedar tree marking the springs and the winters, the lightning's jagged edge and the winding of rivers in photographs taken from the air, all are signs with a message for those who can read them. Those who are moved by looking at these signs but fail to understand, unaware that all nature is written for them, are like the country girl who enjoys the beautiful writing on a letter that has fallen into her hands but has never learned to read and so does not know that these signs are a love letter addressed to her. We too are signs of God. Each one of us bears God's handwriting, and our whole being is a message from God. We have been inscribed into creation (which is itself a divine communication) as the particularly important words, for we are created in the image of God.

We have made gods in our own image and likeness because God first made us in God's image and likeness.

The reason why human love exists is that the human face is an image and likeness of the face of God. We love God in the faces of others. Every human face is veiled, hiding with a veil the one whom we cannot see face to face and live.

We were created for a plural God, a God who spoke in the plural when creating us: "Let us make the human being in our own image and likeness." Every one of us bears the image of this plurality, the Holy Trinity, that is, the image of love. For God is love (between persons) and we were created in the image of a social God.

This image of God in us is the face of Christ. The face of Christ is printed on our faces as it was on Veronica's veil. This face is printed on every lovely thing. St. John Climacus tells the story of a man who, whenever he saw a beautiful woman, burned with the love of God and burst into tears, praising God.

The Jewish people were forbidden to make images of God because humanity is the image of God. And even animals are God's image because they are the image of human beings who are the image of God (and that's why we love animals).

This image of God in us is the face of Christ.

13

The word of God is revealed to us only in silence.

God's image was obscured by sin (devils are faces that have lost God's image), but with Christ it was restored. With Christ we become again the image and word of God, for he is the word and the image of the Father ("Whoever has seen me has seen the Father").

The word of God is revealed to us only in silence.

It is in the depths of every being and deep within us too. We do not have to go far to find it, nor need we travel out of ourselves. We do not have to go far to find happiness; we have only to find ourselves. We have only to descend to our inner depths and find our own identity (which is in God). People nowadays are always trying to get away from themselves. We are unable to be silent or alone, because then we would be by ourselves. So places of entertainment and cinemas are always full. And if we sometimes find ourselves at a point where we might encounter God, we turn on the radio or the television.

Prayer

*Prayer is establishing
contact with God.*

PRAYER is as natural to us as speaking, sighing, or gazing, as natural as the beating of a lover's heart. Prayer is a murmur, a sigh, a glance, and the quickened heartbeat. It is natural to us, an instinct, but in our fallen state it is something we must learn anew, because it has become a forgotten instinct.

Prayer is establishing contact with God. It is a communication with God and as such it does not have to be in words or even articulated mentally. We can communicate by a look, a smile, a sigh, or a gesture. Even smoking can be a prayer, or painting a picture, or looking up at the sky, or drinking water. All our bodily actions are prayers. Our body gives grateful thanks when it is thirsty and drinks a glass of water, or when we plunge into a cool river on a hot day; our very being sings a hymn of thanksgiving to our creator. We may not have given thought to this prayer or even intended it. It may be quite involuntary. But we can turn everything we do into a prayer. Work is an existential prayer. The Lord

15

told St. Angela of Foligno that he was pleased with all her actions, even her eating and drinking and sleeping. He was pleased with her whole being, even her bodily functions.

The Little Flowers of St. Francis tells us that the prayer of Brother Maseo consisted simply of repeating the sound, "Ooh, ooh, ooh!" And that Brother Bernard's prayer consisted in running over the mountains.

God enfolds us like an atmosphere. Just as the atmosphere is full of sight and sound waves that we cannot see or hear except through the proper channels, so we are surrounded by the waves of God, which we cannot pick up except through the proper channels. We cannot pick up God's waves if we live in this world purely through our senses.

We can communicate with one another by way of God, as if by telecommunication through the atmosphere, just as two friends or lovers can communicate even though they are far apart in distant cities. And they can be closer together, in spite of the distance, than two neighbors separated by only a common wall in the same village.

God enfolds us like an atmosphere.

We are so near God that we cannot see God.

But God is also infinitely far from us. We are infinitely distant from God. Union with God is like lovers kissing through a pane of glass.

We see God darkly. God is like a film we can't see on the screen until the doors are shut and the lights out. As the room grows darker, the picture on the screen becomes clearer. Or God is like a house in which all the lights are out except in one inner room; we grope our way through the rooms and along the dark corridors, bumping into furniture, led by the hand of someone who knows the house.

God's presence is also elusive and veiled. And it becomes more so as God comes nearer. It is like a very delicate form of lens, between our sight and reality. We must not use force on it to try to break through. The fact is, we are so near God that we cannot see God.

We do not feel the presence of God because we are ordinarily used to experience coming to us from the outside, whereas this experience comes from within. We are turned outward, dependent on outward sensation, unaccustomed to noticing what is going on within.

We suppose that if God were to speak to us it would

be with a physical voice that would enter our ears from without. Or we confuse God's presence with ourselves, and so fail to recognize God. We do not know that at the very center of our being there is another, that our identity is in another, that turning inward and finding ourselves is to fall into the arms of another.

We are always seeking God's embrace, but we do so in the wrong way — turning outward. We hear the voice of our Beloved, calling us within, and we think it comes from somewhere outside.

God is everywhere, even on Broadway, but we can hear God's voice only in silence.

We can hear God's voice only in silence.

The Secret Chamber

FOR ST. TERESA OF AVILA, life was like a night spent in an uncomfortable inn, just as for Cervantes the castles of human illusions were really humble inns. But for St. Teresa the soul is a castle, like the castles on the plain

The soul is the secret chamber to which only God has the key.

of Castile. And the center of our being, where God is, is the bridal chamber in the castle. For most people, in contrast, it is the dungeon to which they never descend. But it is really the secret dwelling place, the bridal chamber in each one of us.

Love dwells within us. God is crazed with love, and God's behavior is therefore unpredictable. God may do something silly at any time, because, like any lover, God does not reason. God is drunk with love.

The soul is the secret chamber to which only God has the key. And if God does not enter, it remains empty. The senses may be surfeited with pleasure but the soul remains empty.

I have seen Venice and Capri and I was delighted by their beauty, but I was not satisfied. Something was lacking. The dregs of every pleasure were melancholy and anguish. And now my memories are as unreal as picture postcards. It was an empty vision.

All beauty has an element of sadness. Bitterness and distress are in the depths of all things. This is the cosmic cry of which St. Paul speaks. But in us creation rests from its anguish, when our hearts rest in God.

We tire of movies and parties and yachts. But we do not tire of God. Trappists have no need for recreation, for their whole life is recreation. Likewise birds and squirrels do not need playtime, for their whole life, even when they are at work looking for food, is recreation and permanent playtime.

And what would oil or steel magnates give to buy this peace? If they knew about it they would give their whole empires. Just as all those who have ever known about it have given all their possessions. For millionaires seek happiness in money, and they would gladly dispense with money if they knew where happiness was to be found.

Many people grasp the pleasures of the senses with mystical fervor. They are seeking God where God cannot be found, and when they do not find God they become desperate. They may turn to vice or crime, go mad, or commit suicide. They seek happiness in money, in sex, in wine, in nightclubs. They seek it with all the strength of those faculties created for the beatific vision.

Many people are seeking God where God cannot be found.

21

Anguish

*We were created for love,
for a God who is love.*

WE WERE CREATED for love, for a God who is love. And the worst sufferings and the hardest pains of each one of us are caused by love. How many people live a boring and sterile life in this world, loveless, always longing for a love to bring fulfillment, but never finding it. How fully could they satisfy their almost limitless capacity for love, tenderness, and self-surrender, if they would only turn inward to the inexhaustible love that lives and breathes within them. Their lives would be rapturous, they would smile and sigh and take delight in a paradise of love. But their poor lives are without love; they feel the relentless passage of time, spring following spring, as they grow old and still love fails to arrive.

Passion

GOD IS LOVE. And we are also love, because we are made in God's image and likeness. God is love, and, since God is infinitely simple, God must be nothing other than love. If God is infinite good, infinite wisdom, infinite truth, infinite beauty, and infinite justice, this simply means that God is love, which is infinitely good, infinitely wise, infinitely true, infinitely beautiful, and infinitely just. But God is nothing apart from love.

And we who are made in God's image are also nothing but love. Our rational being is one sole desire, one sole passion, the thirst and the cry for love.

All that has not been falsified in us is love. Ontologically we are love. And God, like ourselves, is a cry of love, an infinite passion and infinite thirst for love. This love is the reason for our existence.

And this love of God and our own love are the same love, a love without end, inextinguishable, like the fire of hell. It is a thirst that can never be quenched because the more we drink the more we desire.

God is love. And we are also love, because we are made in God's image and likeness.

23

We are love's invention, and we were created to love.

And in our being and in all our movements we keep alive the memory of the God from whom we came, even when we are far from God. We are like those sea creatures who retain the memory of the sea, even when they have been put in an aquarium, and still go on moving with the rhythm of the waves, no matter their distance from the sea.

God knows no rest until creation, like the prodigal son, returns to him. God longs for us with infinite yearning and the Holy Spirit is the sigh of this longing.

The word of God became flesh for love of us and for love of the Father, so that we can love the Father in ourselves, and God can love God's own self in millions of souls and millions of lives.

We are love's invention, and we were created to love. We are high-tension wires carrying the power of love. Should we fall into self-love, we insulate ourselves from the current. Rather, we should love others as we love ourselves, we should surrender ourselves totally to love and let its power run through us. We should be transmitters of love.

Every created being is in communion with God's be-ing, but in nonrational beings this communion is more imperfect and limited. We are the only creatures in the whole universe capable of love with our conscious being. We are born with aching hearts, like the wounded heart of Jesus. We are not a meaningless passion, as Sartre calls us, but a passion whose meaning is God.

We are not a meaningless passion but a passion whose meaning is God.

Holiness

HOLINESS expresses our true personality. Just as no two leaves are the same, so every person is unique. But sin levels us and makes us uniform. The saints how-ever are all different. They have realized the unique identity to which each of us is called but which we have lost through sin.

The more we identify with God, the more we become truly ourselves. The closer our identification with God, the clearer our own identity — not because our essence is

God's love and beauty impart beauty to the soul.

God, but because our essence is to be the image of God, which is nearly the same thing.

The more we are like God, the more we are ourselves, because our destiny is to be a portrait — a self-portrait — of God. We are not infinite, but we are an image of the infinite, which is nearly the same thing.

We do not know how beautiful the human soul is because we have never seen it. But we have seen the absence of the soul, the corruption of the body from which the soul has departed. From the rotting corpse we can derive an idea, in reverse, of what the soul is. In contrast the beauty of the living body, when the soul is present, can give us an idea of the beauty of the soul apart from the body. Great works of art reflect the soul of the artist, and we glimpse something similar when we draw near the mystery of another human soul in friendship or in love.

God's love and beauty impart beauty to the soul, and the soul that mirrors God is aflame with love. In such a soul, an infinite beauty and an infinite love are reflected as the deep blue sky is mirrored in Lake Nicaragua in May.

The disembodied soul is all smiles and emotion and love, trembling with passion and fire, pure tenderness and feeling, pure vitality and life. And the more the soul is united to God in contemplation, the better it knows God, and the better it knows God, the more it possesses God in love. Its whole life then consists in giving and receiving, ever more enjoying and trembling with love.

Before God the soul is passive and receptive; it cannot take the initiative. The soul cannot approach God unassisted because it does not know where God abides. It must await God's visit, and until God comes, it remains alone. In the meantime, the soul cannot move from where it is. It is rather God who comes and goes, visits and leaves. Neither does the soul know how to caress; it only sometimes very timidly caresses God. But it knows how to let God caress it, and this is all it really knows. The soul does not know how to kiss God, but it receives God's tender and passionate kisses; it allows itself to be kissed and faints with love.

The soul of an old woman is as tender and young and fresh as a child's, because it is the source of life and does not age with the passage of time. And the soul of the

The soul does not know how to kiss God, but it receives God's tender and passionate kisses.

27

God's reflection in opaque matter dazzles us.

coarsest man is as full of light as the soul of Beethoven or Dante. For the soul is the principle of life. It is pure innocence, pure light and joy, lightness, sweetness, and grace. And that is why God is so in love with it. Everyone walking in the street has a soul like this. And it is so sad that this soul gives itself to such inferior loves and is enslaved by food and drink, diversions and money.

Occasionally we glimpse the beauty of the soul in pure eyes, through which some light of the soul shines filtered through dense matter, as sunlight is filtered through closed eyelids.

But while the body is alive, soul and body remain one. The soul is the life and vitality of the body and prevents it becoming a corpse. "If the body is not the soul, what is the soul?" asked Walt Whitman. As Aristotle said, the soul is the substance that gives form to the body.

God's reflection in opaque matter dazzles us. God's reflection is the splendor of all beautiful material things. How much more shall this beauty dazzle us when it is reflected not in opaque matter but revealed in a pure God-like spirit. The essence of all natural beauties, the common denominator of all that is beautiful (in the blue sea, in lakes, in snowy mountains, in deserts, flowers, and stars) is also in the human soul, but there it exists in a more concentrated way, as if it had evolved further, been refined and transformed into a higher beauty that is pure God-like spirit. It is like a concentration of thousands of lovely smiles and beautiful landscapes. And yet it is more than that.

As St. Teresa said, "My daughters, we are not hollow inside."

From all eternity we were chosen from among an infinite number of possible beings.

Chosen

GOD DOES NOT love us *en masse,* but individually. The mere fact of our existence is proof of God's infinite and eternal love, for from all eternity we were chosen from among an infinite number of possible beings. God chose us, not those other possible beings, and so they do not exist. And among all these others God also chose each of us in particular. We were chosen from an infin-

God loves us more than we love ourselves.

ity of other possible beings who might have existed but who were not created. We were the ones chosen from an infinite number of possibilities, and the very fact that we exist is the greatest proof of God's preferential love.

Each of us is irreplaceable. We are all unique collector's pieces because God is an artist who never repeats or copies. No two leaves are alike, no two fingerprints are the same, and even less are any two souls identical. God does not reproduce the lost soul; it is lost for all eternity, and God feels the loss forever.

God loves us more than we love ourselves. God loves us as only God can love, as God loves God's own self. How bitter will be God's disappointment if God is eternally separated from any one of us.

God is love. And God's love is often unrequited. This is a bitter tragedy. Sometimes God appears to be a tyrant demanding more and more of us, but this is simply love beseeching. The creator of the universe begs for your love!

God loves each and every one of us as if there were only the two of us in the whole universe. God does not need humans in order to be happy, but God loves us as if he would be eternally unhappy without us. Although God has lived from all eternity without needing human beings, God humiliates himself like a slave for love of us, as if he could not live without us. God loves the human soul so much, says St. Catherine of Genoa, that it is as if God were a slave and the soul were God.

Sometimes it seems as if God has forgotten all the rest of the universe and wants only to converse with us.

Like a lover who spends all his time thinking of his distant love, God has been thinking of me since before I was born, for all eternity.

And we also long for God; we are homesick for our creator from the time we are born. Existence for us is exile, far from God. God is love, and we who are made in God's image, are also love. Every cell in our body is love, made for love, as the grain of incense is made for the fire. And our whole being is ready to burn in this fire.

The one thing that separates us from God is selfishness, self-love. So our union with God can only be through the death of self. Either God or me. As soon as our self surrenders within us, God enters in.

We have only to repeat Mary's fiat for God to be in-

God has been thinking of me since before I was born, for all eternity.

31

Is there any greater joy than to love and be loved?

carnate again in us. A transubstantiation takes place in us as in the bread and wine, and our flesh and blood are changed into Christ, the flesh and blood of God. We become a eucharist, a sacrifice of love.

For St. Bernard this mystical union is a mutual exchange. God becomes the soul and the soul becomes God. Love always makes two things into one. Here on earth two beings never become completely one. Only God becomes one with the soul, without ceasing to be God.

True Center

GOD IS LOVE. And is there any greater joy than to love and be loved? God is God because God is love, because he is the joy of love. God is the infinite joy of infinite love.

And everything that exists sprang from this love. All things were made by love and all things are love.

God would not have created a single thing had he hated it, as the Book of Wisdom says (11:24–25), and the mere fact that God sustains it is proof of God's love. The existence of all things is due to God's love, God's loving kiss.

Picasso was right when he said that we do not know what a tree or a window really is. All things are very mysterious and strange (like Picasso's paintings), and we overlook their strangeness and their mystery only because we are so used to them. Only dimly do we understand the nature of things. What are things? They are God's love become things.

God also communicates with us by way of all things. They are messages of love. When I read a book, God is speaking to me through this book. I raise my eyes to look at the countryside: God created it for me to see. The picture I look at today was inspired by God in the painter, for me to see. Everything I enjoy was given lovingly by God for me to enjoy, and even my pain is God's loving gift.

God's love created the world and continues creating it at every moment through the process of evolution. Be-

When I read a book, God is speaking to me through this book.

33

God established the law of evolution.

cause God the creator is also master of evolution, the world's evolution is the work of God's love. When God said, "Increase and multiply," God established the law of evolution.

The world is not like a picture painted by an artist centuries ago that now hangs untouchable in a museum. It is more like a work of art in constant progress, still in the artist's studio.

God is not made of marble, as St. Paul told the Athenians on the Areopagus when he gazed on their marble statues. God is not a statue at all, but the living God in whom "we live and move and have our being." From God came the marble on the Areopagus as well as the hand that worked the marble and the inspiration that moved the hand.

We all make ourselves the center of the universe and therefore live in a false universe, like the universe of astronomers before Copernicus. Things interest us to the extent that they serve our own small interests. But we can be happy only if God is the center of our universe. Then we will rejoice in everything that exists and be glad that things are as they are and that everything happens as it does. For God wants it so, whether or not it is convenient to our own little notions.

God is love, but our own self-love is the opposite of love. The refusal of self-giving, it is love turned inward; it is actually hate.

We find it difficult to love others as we love ourselves; it is difficult for us even to conceive of such love. But this will be our natural state in heaven, for the heavenly state *is* our natural state. Humanity was created as an organic whole, even though it is made up of individuals. "So God created the human being in his own image, in the image of God he created him; male and female he created them" (Gen. 1:27).

Humanity is a single body comprising many individuals. Individual self-love is unnatural, as is the self-love of one cell in our own body. When one cell puts itself first and before the organic functioning of the whole body, when it declares war on the other cells, this is cancer. Self-love is the cancer of the whole mystical body. As St. Paul says, "The eye cannot say to the hand, 'I have no need of you,' nor again the head to the feet, 'I have no need of you'" (1 Cor. 12:21).

Our own self-love is the opposite of love.

Providence

God's love is the water we drink, the air we breathe, and the light we see.

ALL NATURE is charity, but only the mystic experiences this love completely. The love of God surrounds us. God's love is the water we drink, the air we breathe, and the light we see. All natural phenomena are different material forms of the love of God. We move in God's love as the fish swims in water. And we are so close to God, so wrapped in God's love and showered with God's gifts (we ourselves are God's gift) that we do not realize it, lacking perspective. God's love surrounds us, but we do not feel it any more than we feel the pressure of the atmosphere.

Nature is God's love made perceptible to the senses in material form. God's providence is visible in all that we see. People hurry through the streets preoccupied and never stop for a moment to think of God or to remember that in God they move, that God surrounds them and that every hair of their heads is counted, every cell in their body is numbered. Why are we so preoccupied?

37

God hears the cry of the deer in the valley calling for a mate. And God answers that cry.

Why do we go through cities frowning and preoccupied, as if each of us were alone in a strange and hostile world? Why do we fuss about what we eat and drink and wear and what brand we should buy? Consider the birds of the air and lilies of the field. Consider the sea anemone and the humble protozoan. They neither sow nor reap; they have neither barns nor bank accounts nor life insurance.

God, in his providence, has taken care of the earth for billions of years, but still we feel strange and lonely in the universe, preoccupied with our affairs as if there were no one to care for us. We forget that Another is taking care of every fiber of our being at every moment, governing the flow of our blood and the functioning of our organs. And yet we believe there is no one but ourselves in the whole universe who can solve a small problem in our practical life.

God hears the cry of the deer in the valley calling for a mate. And God answers that cry. God cares for the cuckoo demanding food. God guides the swans in their migrations. When the weasel and the badger sleep in the early morning, God watches over them. The little frog, the beetle, and the raven all find food in due time each day.

> These all look to thee,
> to give them their food in due season.
> When thou givest to them, they gather it up;
> when thou openest thy hand, they are filled with
>   good things.

(Ps. 104:27–28)

Every human being is born with a heart touched by love.

God and Nothing

EVERY HUMAN BEING is born with a heart touched by love and with a powerful thirst. "My soul thirsts for thee like a parched land" (Ps. 143). God created eating and drinking as material symbols of this love.

This thirst for God is the anxiety on all the faces of all the people walking in the street, going into shops, cinemas, and bars. Everyone wants things, many things,

The desire for possession is like an incurable disease.

an infinity of things: one more glass, one more sweet, one more look, one more word, one more kiss, one more book, one more journey. Always the craving for more. Human faces are racked with anxiety and desire. We who have escaped from this slavery are like prisoners who have escaped from concentration camps or forced labor.

We may think that just a little more will do, that contentment will come with a small house and a car, a lovely family. But we always go out into the street with the same anxious face, seeking new things with the same eagerness, always dissatisfied. The desire for possession is like an incurable disease.

As Plato says, the human body is a cracked vase that cannot be filled. The senses may be surfeited with pleasures, but the soul remains hungry. The body's pleasures have not reached it and have only made its mouth water, as though the longed-for cup had never touched its lips.

It is like trying to satisfy ourselves with food that does not nourish or wine that does not warm us. Food fills us and wine excites us, but they do not satisfy our deepest need.

And just as we realize the depth of a well when we throw a stone in and do not hear it hit the water, we realize how deep our soul must be when things drop into it and disappear without us hearing them hit the bottom.

Because God is in the depths of every soul, its depths are infinite and nothing can fill them but God. A wine that satisfied us completely would have to share in the infinite, like the water that Christ offered to the Samaritan woman by the well. That water is such a wine.

But in monasteries we see human beings who are fulfilled and content. They smile and do not have anxious frowns on their faces. Ignatius of Loyola said that if he were forced to dissolve his Society, he would regain the same inner peace in fifteen minutes.

Animals are also peaceful. They do not go about anxiously, but are quiet and content like monks.

Human beings are never satisfied with earthly things because they were not created for things of the earth. Animals satisfy their needs and want nothing more. They do not thirst for the infinite. This earth is their heaven. So animals are not disappointed by life and never commit suicide, because they were created for this

Human beings are never satisfied with earthly things because they were not created for things of the earth.

41

earth. (Thus all animals are saints with an animal sanctity; they are chaste, poor, and obedient like humble monks.)

But our whole being is designed to love God and to be with God and enjoy God, just as the mackerel's body is made to swim through the water and the body of the seagull to fly over the sea.

Just as a telephone is designed for telephonic conversation and not for anything else, human beings were not made to enjoy this life but to enjoy God and to love God and so we can be truly happy only with God.

And although we have not seen God, we are like migrating birds or fishes who were born in a strange place but who, when winter comes, feel a mysterious restlessness in the blood, a longing for another warmer country that they have never seen. They set out for it without knowing where it is. They have felt the call of the promised land. They hear a beloved voice calling: "Arise, my love, my fair one and come away; for lo the winter is past, the rain is over and gone" (Song of Songs 2:10).

The human soul is born in love, but it does not see the

one it loves. That One is reflected in all created things, and so we cling to them. The infant eagerly stretches out its tiny arms toward everything it sees; it tries to put everything it touches in its mouth and wants to touch and pick up everything. Later on it clings to its toys, and even when it is finally grown up the desire to cling to things remains the same. But we are never satisfied unless one day we leave hold of things and turn instead to God.

But God can be found only in nothingness, for God is found only where no things are. Things can never be fully possessed, and so they leave us always unsatisfied.

"O world, never to be able to embrace you wholly!" exclaims the poet Edna St. Vincent Millay. This is the pain of the human heart. It longs to possess the world but cannot. (Alexander wept because he could not conquer the stars.) In love we long to possess another human body, but here too we are ultimately frustrated. Only God can be totally embraced, because the arms of our soul were made to embrace the infinite and nothing less.

We can fully embrace neither the world nor other hu-

Only God can be totally embraced, because the arms of our soul were made to embrace the infinite and nothing less.

Loving God is now my only reason for living, my only profession, my only occupation.

mans, and they cannot return our embrace. Only God can satisfy our longing.

God gives us the joy of pleasure and the headiness of wine without the need for drinking. God is the infinite sum of all pleasures, of joys, and delights, and love, not like the mere shadows of pleasures, joy, and delight, the shadows of love that we avidly pursue.

In God is the beauty of every human face, the savor of all fruit, the power of all wine, and the sweetness and bitterness of all earthly loves. To taste one drop of God turns our head forever.

Someone who has tasted one drop of this bliss cannot go on living as before, going to the office every morning and keeping up with social conventions. One goes mad and breaks all the rules. One may walk the street in rags or wearing a dunce's cap, attracting the laughter of passersby. One may preach in the streets or shut oneself up in a cell for the rest of life, or even resort to kissing lepers. People call it a "conversion."

Loving God is now my only reason for living, my only profession, my only occupation. I have surrendered to God as passionately as I used to surrender to human beauty, and I know that God will love me and satisfy me as no other ever could. And I know I will find in God the well-remembered features of all those beautiful faces I once loved. I love God with the love I had for all God's handiwork. My love has remained but its object is not the same. The burning thirst, the desert heat, the almost cosmic hunger for love, the insatiable longing, the empty heart remain. All my former loves have died. Now I love only God, with all my love. Lord, have pity on my empty heart.

I love God with the love I had for all God's handiwork.

Infinity

GOD IS LOVE. But love is always love of something or someone. God is love of what? Love of God, naturally. But love of God, who is love, is love of love. Love of a love that is also love of love and so on, *ad infinitum.* This is why God is infinite. God is infinite love of infinite love, or an infinite mutuality of love.

To love God is to share in God.

God is mutual. God is one and also two — two in one — and this mutual union of the two is also God, and so God is also three and one. Love of love, God is love loving itself, much like a mirror reflected in another mirror makes an infinite number of reflections.

God is three because God is love: an infinite projection, procreation, and transmission of himself and outpouring in love. God is one because God is love, unity, self-identity, and communion of the lover and the beloved embracing in love.

And to love God is to share in God, because God is this love of himself. God's love is not a matter of selfishness but of self-surrender, for God is not self-love but mutual love.

And to love others is also to share in God. For what we love in others is the divine spark within them. And it is the same divine spark within us that prompts our love. And what others love in us is what is God-like. So all mutual love resembles the mutual love of the triune God.

Those who love each other give one another a gift that is the very substance of God. If God were unity alone,

God would be all alone, begetting nothing, and so a loveless and sterile God. But God is unity in distinctness. All that is distinct, all plurality in creation comes from God. So does the individuality and unity in all things. The union of one with another is an image of God's union. And our union of all with Christ is a sharing in the union of the Trinity.

God's love of himself is not selfish; it is the love of one person for another, for an infinite other. There is an infinite distinction between the two persons, and the love between them is yet another infinite person who is also God. And the Son loves the Father through us, as if we were an electric cable. When there is no selfishness in us he loves God through us with a love that is God, that is the Holy Spirit, "the Spirit of our Lord Jesus Christ," as Paul says.

The Holy Spirit is the love between the Father and Son, its inspiration, breath, and kiss. The Son is the word of God, and the Holy Spirit is God's sigh, the sound of God's love. The Son is the projection and expression of God, God's conversation, and the Holy Spirit is the sigh of two lovers.

The Son is the word of God, and the Holy Spirit is God's sigh, the sound of God's love.

47

God is above all numbers, as God's name (the Word) is above every other name.

This is the dogma of love, the dogma of the Holy Trinity, the mystery that God is not alone, that God is union and communion.

St. Ignatius of Loyola was moved to tears in the streets of Rome whenever he saw three of anything — three pigeons, three men, three stars in the sky, three children playing — because they reminded him of this mystery of the Trinity. The Trinity is love. Every human family with a father, mother, and child is an image of the Trinity. So is all fertility in nature, for in nature too everything is trinitarian; all things come from other things, and each thing joins with another to make two, while a third is born of their union.

God is three and one, but his number is not that of our counting: 1,2,3,4. God is an infinite one and an infinite three, and in God all numbers and all unity are contained.

God is above all numbers, as God's name (the Word) is above every other name. Every other word and every other name stand for or symbolize something else. The infinite Word not only stands for or symbolizes something else but is the thing itself, which is infinite. It is the infinite name of an infinite reality, and the name is the reality itself. When God disclosed his name, he said, "I Am Who I Am," that is, the one whose very existence is his name. Or the one who has no name but simply exists. Or the one whose name is simply existence. And this is the name the Father gave his Son, "a name which is above every other name," as Paul says, above our semantics and beyond all language: "This glorious and awful name, the LORD your God" (Deut. 28:58).

God is Nothing in comparison with things.

Atheism

THE ATHEIST who denies the existence of God proclaims a partial truth — namely, the fact that God does not exist in the sense that other things exist. Theologians call this God's "transcendence." Denis the Areopagite, Meister Eckhart, Henry Suso, and other mystics also call God the Nothing, the Great Nothing. For God is no-thing as other things are; God is Nothing in compar-

God is not only light but darkness.

ison with things. God is a non-being. And if existence is what we call the underlying property of all things, then, in strict terms, God does not exist. On the other hand, if existence is how we name God, then nothing else truly exists. God is simply so different from everything else that it is as if God did not exist. Or if God exists, everything else is nothing in God's sight. So in a certain sense God does not exist, and again in a certain sense God alone exists.

And the atheists are also right, in a certain sense, to deny God, if God is conceived anthropomorphically. Such a God does indeed not exist and is no more than a fairy tale. But if they intuit the existence of something vague, incomprehensible, and mysterious, without knowing what it is nor what it is called, they are also darkly affirming the existence of God, a being they can neither understand nor imagine, whom no person can look upon and live. Their God is also the Unknown God of whom St. Paul spoke on the Areopagus in Athens. St. Paul told the Athenians that the Unknown God was the true God whom they worshiped without knowing it.

God is not only light but darkness. The idea of "nothingness" that atheists ascribe to God is the same nothingness that the mystics know by experience. They have had personal experience of this nothingness; they have proved its bottomless abyss of sweetness and love and have felt its tender embrace.

God is simultaneously light and darkness, or, better, God is neither light nor darkness, but when God created the world he separated the light from the darkness for us and made us "children of light." We cannot possess the full knowledge of good and evil, but only the knowledge of good, for we were created in light, together with everything else. God alone has the full knowledge of good and evil. Mystical experience is experience of this darkness in God, or of God's reality where there is no separation of light and darkness, from which came both day and night. For God is also the creator of night, and God is also night. Night of love and mystery. And we who came from this night also long for this beautiful darkness.

God is infinitely beautiful, but we could also say that there is within God a certain "ugliness," for God's beauty is beyond all our notions of beauty. "To create

For God is also the creator of night, and God is also night.

51

God also has a sense of humor.

something new you always have to make it ugly," Picasso said. And God is infinite newness. As St. Paul says, we know the invisible perfection of God by means of the visible world. The fascinating beauty of certain reptiles and insects, monsters of the deep and weird creatures of the microcosmos suggests something of what the terrible, eternally new, and revolutionary beauty of God might be like.

And God also has a sense of humor, an infinite one. We know God's invisible perfection through the visible world; the green lizard, the rabbit, the locust, the protozoan, the praying mantis, kneeling on its outsize knees as if it were in prayer—all these suggest something about God's sense of humor.

God is not only infinitely great but, as Denis the Areopagite says, "God is also small." God is infinitely small. And just as we get a conception of the infinite greatness of God by looking at the macrocosm through a telescope, we can also discover God's infinite littleness by looking at the microcosm through a microscope. And if the starry sky or the sea proclaim the grandeur of God, the eyes of insects and the ant's digestive system proclaim God's lowliness. For if we can say that God is greater than the whole universe, we can also say that God is smaller than an electron.

"Everything you say of him is false," says Meister Eckhart.

At times our vision and God's become one, as if God were in our eyes.

Looking

SOMETIMES WE FEEL God looking at us intently, infinitely, with an infinite intensity fixed from all eternity. At other times we feel we are looking at God, opening wide the eyes of our soul, our whole self concentrated in our gaze, and our vision and God's become one, as if God were in our eyes, the lover and the beloved together. At other times the little soul feels God's embrace or feels itself embracing God. Sometimes it merely clutches the air but at other times feels a certain contact with God. Sometimes the sensation is like the gentlest of caresses, ruffling the soul and the skin with a

delicious excitement (for "if the soul is not the body, what is the soul?"). Sometimes our whole self yearns, we become pure longing, loving with each heartbeat and each breath, with every cell and gland and organ, pulsing with a love that rises and falls in constant rhythm.

At night the soul sleeps smiling and confident, knowing that it is loved and cherished by the Beloved. Sometimes it wakes in the night from the sensation of a kiss, and the impression of a face, like the image on Veronica's veil.

Today I looked at You with sad and tearful eyes, the hungry eyes of my soul, You the source of all the beauties in the world, which are reflections of your beauty, and of all the loves in the world which are reflections of Your love: the light in the lover's eyes at the sight of the beloved, love of two birds together, the love of all human beings and all animals. We are alone in the chapel, You and I, while outside the world's traffic passes by. At these moments I have nothing and no one. I am totally dispossessed and alone in the world. But I have everything, I am happy, I lack nothing, want nothing. Because what others seek in a woman or a family, in

We are alone in the chapel, You and I, while outside the world's traffic passes by.

All my life is here, and all my world and all my loves.

friends, at parties, I have here. What the poet seeks in poetry and the painter in painting I have here. What the dictator seeks in power and the rich man in money and the drunkard in wine, and what I too used to search for in vain, I have right here. All my life is here, and all my world and all my loves. I have all this great wealth, while possessing nothing. I have all this joy, all peace, all beauty, and all love. I am satisfied and want nothing else. For I have You, and so I have all things, for You are lord of all — all stars, all nations, and all beings on earth.

My liver, my brain, my heart, all my organs and glands exist in order to love You. Everything on earth, all poetry, the loveliness of faces, the countryside, friendship, the day and the night were created that I might love You.

That I should love You with all my heart, with all my mind, with my imagination, with all the tenderness that is in me, with all the feeling and the poetry that is in me. That I should love You with all my passions and appetites and all my strength. And also with all my sweetness, all the passion and fire and longing for possession with which I used to love creatures. These creatures were tyrants over me. "My mother's sons were angry with me, they made me keeper of the vineyards; but my own vineyard I have not kept" (Song of Solomon 1:6).

The soul tries to hide and vanish from God's presence but cannot.

Unending Moment

S UDDENLY THE SOUL feels God's unmistakable presence and cries out with trembling fear: "It's You who made heaven and earth!" The soul tries to hide and vanish from God's presence but cannot. It cannot get away, for God is all around, and there is nowhere to escape, for God is present throughout heaven and earth. The soul itself is in God's arms. Having run after happiness and never found it, having sought after beauty, pleasure, and joy without satisfaction, the soul is now overwhelmed by an ocean of delight, boundless and fathomless. It is too much. It cries: "Enough, enough. If You love me give me no more of this joy or I shall die." The soul is penetrated by such an intense sweetness that it feels like

We all have within us a secret place, a locked room, an inner paradise created for love.

pain, an indescribable pain, at once infinitely bitter and infinitely sweet. Sometimes this can all happen in a moment, never to reoccur in a whole lifetime. But after this experience all the beauties and pleasures and joys of the earth seem empty. They are as "dung," as the saints have said. Now the soul can no longer enjoy anything else but what it had at that moment, so that henceforth life will be torture and martyrdom. Made with love, overcome with the joy it has once known, the soul will suffer torments till it tastes this presence a second time.

Inner Depths

EVERYONE HAS an inner room. Deep inside every human being there is a bridal chamber where only the bridegroom comes. We all have within us a secret place, a locked room, an inner paradise created for love. But most people do not know it is there.

So most people have an inner loveless emptiness. For

human love, at its deepest, never reaches this sanctuary. It is the inner room, the place of which the bride speaks in the Song of Songs: "He took me into his chamber." Outside the bridegroom is knocking, as we read in the Book of Revelation: "Behold I stand at the door and knock. If anyone hears my voice and opens the door, I will go in and sup with him and he with me."

In the depths of our being everyone hears this call. It is the plaintive voice that Nietzsche heard in his heart and that caused him pain and fear. It is the voice in the Song of Songs: "Open to me, my sister, my love, my dove, my perfect one; for my head is wet with dew, my locks with the drops of the night." But the bride answers from her bed, "I have put off my garment, how can I put it on? I have bathed my feet, how can I soil them?"

In their deepest being, most people have an empty room. Sometimes they hear a painful voice crying in the silence of the night or the sound of someone knocking at the door. There is a sadness within most people, though outside they may smile and be merry.

The presence of love is within us, and yet we are alone. If we turn inward, we will find it. But we do not

There is a sadness within most people, though outside they may smile and be merry.

We were created for love, to love our Creator. And time not dedicated to this love is time wasted.

know it because first we would have to go through the agony of giving up everything, even ourselves. Our Beloved is calling to us from deep within or, rather, in our inmost depth, so deep that we think it comes from beyond. He is deeper than our own consciousness or our dreams.

And we are terrified of being alone. In the train or the doctor's waiting room or wherever we may be, we are terrified of being alone, without a book or a paper to read, with nothing to see or do or say. And all the while our best friend is knocking outside, his head moist with dew.

We were created for love, to love our Creator. And time not dedicated to this love is time wasted.

Love is the one law that rules the universe, the law, as Dante said, that moves the sun and the other stars. It is the law by which all things cohere. It is the very substance of the universe. Each body in the universe attracts every other body by the force of its gravity. The earth attracts to itself every object on the earth and all these objects mutually attract one another. The earth attracts the moon and the sun attracts the earth, the moon, and the other planets, and all the other stars in heaven, even the most distant. And all these other stars attract the sun and the planets and the earth and everything on the earth and all the other stars, each pulling strongly and each in its own way. And every particle of matter in the universe attracts every other particle of matter. Even when two bodies are in an absolute vacuum, with no connection between them, we know that they are strongly attracted to one another. To love is to seek union. It is our only joy.

Every soul that God creates is created for love. This was the restlessness that filled Augustine's heart, until he finally understood for whom his heart yearned and whom he loved.

God is this great feeling of solitude with which we are all born, along with the consciousness that there exists a partner.

And this friend is within us, in the place where our dreams reside, in the darkness of our subconscious, in the depths of our personality. God is in our secret self that we reveal to no one, not even to husband or wife, not even to ourselves. At the source of dreams, of myths,

To love is to seek union. It is our only joy.

Apart from God the bitter wind of loneliness blows through us.

of love, there the Beloved has his bridal chamber. When this chamber is empty, we are filled with loneliness, fear, melancholy, and boredom. We may have a lot of money and property, securities in the bank, and our house in order, but in ourselves we can remain empty. Apart from God the bitter wind of loneliness blows through us. Sometimes at night the soul, deprived so long of God's caress (sometimes after a night of pleasure), wakes in terror at its own loneliness. At other times it wakes in the middle of the night and weeps.

Call

WHAT WE REGARD as reality, the reality we receive through our senses, is like a motion picture. It is real but with the reality of a motion picture. Outside there is another reality. A film can inspire us to love and make us weep and forget that outside there is daylight, spring, genuine love, and the voice of our Beloved who calls in springtime: "Arise my love and come, for the winter is over and gone."

Yet this reality we do not perceive through our senses, but only in the darkness of faith. This reality is like the electric current that invisibly powers and illuminates our lamps. And this voice is like the waves of silent music that are transmitted through space over great distances.

We want God's voice to be clear, but it is not.

We want God's voice to be clear, but it is not. We do not hear it clearly because it cannot be heard by our senses. It is a deep, subtle, and mysterious voice — like a deep yearning within us, at the root of the soul. It is the voice in the night, a voice that calls us. We hear but do not see. We want it to be clear as day but it is deep as night. It is deep and clear, but with a dark clarity like an X-ray. It reaches our bones.

For the voice of our Beloved is existential, not verbal. It does not sound in our ears or in our minds, but deeper, where God is present, in our deepest self. God's call makes us discontented and sick of everything. God does not call us by words, but by events, circumstances, reality. Because this call is not superficial, it does not

God's voice is like the voice of the bird we hear in the night; it calls out without cease.

sound clear to us, for we live only on the surface of ourselves, and we communicate with one another in words. This call is deep, because God dwells in the depths of our being, and so God's voice is silence.

God's call, our vocation, is twofold in meaning. God's call is saying, "Come and follow me." This implies both an arrival and departure, both an encounter and an ongoing search. As St. Gregory of Nyssa says, "To find God is to seek him incessantly." God's call is an incessant call, to the unknown, to adventure, to follow him in the night, in solitude. It is a call incessantly to go further and further. It is not static but dynamic (as God's creation is also dynamic), and reaching God means going ever onward. God's call is like the call to become an explorer; it is an invitation to adventure.

God's voice is like the voice of the bird we hear in the night; it calls out without cease. And another bird answers it much farther away. One bird comes nearer, and the other goes further off, still calling and calling. Then the voices of both birds fade and are lost in the night.

Pleasure

Human beings can be satisfied only with the infinite.

PLEASURE IS a false god who tells us: surrender to me and I will satisfy you. But we can never be satisfied by this god because it is smaller than our soul. We cannot be satisfied with a pleasure that is less than infinite. We are leaking vases. Nor can we be satisfied with a beauty less than infinite, and every beauty that is not God is limited. "In all perfection I saw a limit," cries the psalmist. This is why beautiful things give us that deep feeling of melancholy, a painful sweetness.

Animals are satisfied with created things. They want nothing else. But human beings can be satisfied only with the infinite.

Every instinct in nature demands its rational satisfaction, and every natural need must be met. We are born with an instinct for the infinite, an instinct for God, and this instinct must be satisfied. This is the "thirst for infinite illusions," of which the Nicaraguan poet Rubén Darío spoke.

Clinging to creatures brings frustration, a frustration

God is present in all things, setting them afire without consuming them, like Moses' burning bush.

as deep as that of the dictator deprived of power. It is a clinging to something that does not belong to us, that we unjustly seek to dominate but that is snatched from our grasp.

But when we have tasted God we no longer desire the pleasure that comes from creatures. In the same way, at a banquet we would be repelled by the maggoty bread we might welcome in the concentration camp.

This light of truth, the light of what is real and authentic, which shines and attracts us in all things, is God's light. (Because God is infinite truth, God is infinite splendor.) The soft light of goodness that glows in all things and the brilliant light of beauty, which also attracts us in all things — these are also God's light.

From God all stars derive their light. God is present in all things, setting them afire without consuming them, like Moses' burning bush.

In the presence of anything beautiful — a beautiful woman, for example — you should think of the infinite beauty of your Beloved, the Creator of all beauty on earth, and you should delight in the fact that this beauty glorifies your God. You should not want to possess this beauty or take it away from your Beloved, since he exists for you and you exist for him. Be glad at all this beauty because it is a hymn of praise to your Beloved, and therefore a hymn of praise to you. For you are your Beloved's and he is yours.

The earth is beautiful in every place — whether Nicaragua, Venice, Kentucky, the Sahara. The sea is beautiful and so are the desert, woods, plains, lakes, mountains, the tropics, and the arctic. For everywhere God surrounds us with beauty and poetry, revealing to our eyes and all our senses the beauty of creation, the reflection and splendor of God's invisible beauty.

All God's earth is beautiful, all its corners are delightful, and all its creatures are enchanting. But how are we to renounce this enchantment for the sake of God, who is much more than the sum of all these things? And if the earth so charms us how are we to yearn to see God face to face?

I would go on foot to the ends of the earth if I thought I would meet You there. But You are within me and not at the ends of the earth.

You are within me and in Your eyes are the eyes of all

I would go on foot to the ends of the earth if I thought I would meet You there.

Those who have felt the love of God retire into silence and solitude.

those I have loved and all who have loved me. In Your eyes are reflected all the loving glances that have met my eyes in the world. But Your eyes are fixed on me from all eternity; from all eternity they have been looking at me.

Alone Together

WHOEVER LOVES GOD wishes to be alone. Like newlyweds who do not want to have their intimacy interrupted by outsiders, those who have felt the love of God retire into silence and solitude.

"The soul cannot live without love," says St. Catherine of Siena. If it is not God whom we love we invest our love in other things. Our love for God is the same as the love we previously felt for other things. But whoever loves God alone loves God with the love previously reserved for a thousand other things, and with the strength of someone who loves only one thing in all the world, with a total and universal love.

Love is someone else dwelling within our person. Love is a presence. It is feeling that we belong to someone else and that someone else belongs to us. In love we are two, and yet the two are one. Love is knowing that we are loved, feeling the presence of the other loving us and smiling at us. Love is wanting to be someone else and knowing that we are someone else and that someone else wants to be us and is one with us. Love is being emptied of ourselves and full of another. When we look at our Beloved, our whole soul is in our gaze. When we sigh, our whole soul is in our sigh. It is knowing that we make a pair and feeling at one with every pair we see, two lovers, two clouds, two doves flying past, two stars.

My feeling of solitude and my sighing in the night used to find no echo. It fell upon emptiness. I was alone. But now my sigh has found an echo; it reaches Someone who hears it, Someone I can neither see nor hear in the darkness, but whose answering sigh wells up within me, deeper within me than I am myself.

And this someone is God. I understand Your love and that You forgive me everything, for, like You, I have known what it means to love, to forgive everything —

*Love is being emptied of
ourselves and full
of another.*

69

God loves me with all my weaknesses.

even seventy times seven. My former loves have taught me what love is. I know what it is to be passionately and madly in love with another, and so I have some feeling for God's love for me.

God loves me with all my weaknesses, with all my inherited and acquired defects. God loves me as I am, with my idiosyncrasies and my temperament, my habits and my complexes. Just as I am.

My soul is open. Someone else, not I, has the key. He comes and goes as he pleases.

Marriage

"T HE KINGDOM of heaven is like a king who was making a wedding feast for his son. . . . "

In heaven there will be no giving in marriage, said Christ. That is, there will be no marriages between human couples because there will be no further need for procreation (the mystical body will be complete) and because there will be only one marriage: the wedding of the Lamb.

Heaven is marriage, while hell is disappointed love. Human marriage is an image, a "type" of heaven.

Sex is a symbol of divine love. It is a symbol and sacrament, and its every profanation is a sacrilege. As sacrament and symbol, it transcends its own material reality. It is more than it appears. It signifies a higher reality, the fullness of divine love. That is why a Carthusian once said that monks renounce marriage in favor of what marriage signifies.

The Song of Songs may have been originally a poem of human love (it must at least have been based on a human nuptial song). But divine inspiration transformed it into a symbolization of divine love. For all sexual love symbolizes divine love. And each love poem ever written and each human love (and even the irrational love of animals, the fertility of plants, and the cohesive force of inanimate matter) are figures and types of divine love.

Marriage is so wonderful, so divine for us, because it is the image of the divine marriage.

Heaven is marriage, while hell is disappointed love.

To love God is to possess God. To love God is to be wedded to God.

Sometimes people think there is a dilemma in the choice between consecration to God and marriage. They do not know that consecration to God is itself marriage and that, as St. Bernard says, the person who loves God "marries" God.

The erotic life of the monk has been crucified and resurrected. It still exists but it has been transformed. The monk is pure passion, the passion and madness of love.

In every human desire, in every human appetite, there is a huge quantity of energy, passion, and fire. And how great is this energy and fire when the soul surrenders entirely to the desire and love for one thing alone.

All passions, appetites, feelings, instincts, and every yearning of the human heart are fuel for the love of God. Actually, the entire human being is such a fuel. And the love with which God responds to us is like throwing oil onto a blazing fire.

When we feel we are loved by the one we love, our love is intensified. When we think about the beloved our love is increased, and with this increase in love we think

To love God is to possess God. To love God is to be wedded to God.

Anyone who has ever been madly in love can understand God's love.

about our beloved more, until we are nothing but one burning flame of love.

Every cell in our body, every particle of our being is "nuptial," because we were made for marriage. All that Freud called the "libido" is the oil within the lamps of the wise virgins, who live in expectation of the bridegroom.

St. Maria Magdalena de Pazzi used to run through the corridors of her convent screaming wildly with love: "Love! Love! Do you realize, my sisters, that Jesus is love and that he is mad with love?"

Anyone who has ever been madly in love can understand God's love. Divine love and human love are the same; only their object is different. The religious life is all about love.

Religious do not renounce God's creatures because they are bad, but rather because they are in fact good and beautiful. They are so good and beautiful that they have made us fall in love with their creator. We know the Creator's beauty through the beauty of his creatures; apart from them we have no other way of knowing his beauty.

If we have deprived ourselves of human beauty and human love, it is not because we despise them, but because they have inflamed us with the love of God. Is it not God who created sex, every tender and passionate embrace? The Creator of all things is not a barren God. As Isaiah says, " 'Will I open the mother's womb for no children to be born?' says the Lord. 'Will I close the womb, I who bring all things to birth?' says your God."

God is eternally young and new. God's works are always fresh, and the world is reborn each morning as if it were newly created. Every dawn repeats God's word, "Let there be light," and has the freshness and newness of that first dawn. Through God, each morning, the young colts leap with joy, the doves rejoice, and the mockingbirds sing of God "who is the joy of my youth." The charm and innocence of all young creatures come from God, source of both virginity and fertility. God is the only love who never grows old, is never unfaithful, and never dies.

The Creator of all things is not a barren God.

In the solitude of each soul that is betrothed to Christ, Christ is complete.

Youth

YOUTH IS the time to surrender to God, for it is the time of illusions. Surrendering to God is surrendering in love. And at the age when you have the most dreams and illusions ("a thirst for infinite illusions") the greater is the gift you offer, the greater is the gift you receive, and the greater is the mutual love you share. If you were disappointed with your life, what life would you have to offer? God welcomes youth, fervor, passion, and dreams. God's love is a proposal of marriage, and God asks from you a response in kind.

The marriage in question is of the whole church with Christ and of each particular soul with Christ, for in each soul the whole church is present, just as the body of Christ is complete in each eucharistic host and in the bodies of all Christians. So in a hermit's cave the whole church is present — militant, suffering, and triumphant. And in the solitude of each soul that is betrothed to Christ, Christ is complete. And as all men and women are united in Christ, so in each soul that marries Christ,

Christ is present along with all men and women — that is, the whole mystical body of Christ, "the whole Christ," as St. Augustine says.

Creation is transparent as glass, and the splendor of God shines through it.

Journey

TRYING TO FIND our Creator, we turn instead toward creatures, like the moth that bumps into the window pane. For creation is transparent as glass, and the splendor of God shines through it.

We are attracted by the beauty of created things, little realizing that they are but a reflection of the real beauty. The real beauty is within us. And so, paradoxically, the more we turn outward in pursuit of beauty, the more we turn away from it. For it is in the opposite direction.

But we cannot first be joined to God and then detach ourselves from all created things. First we must leave all things behind, and then we can be joined to God.

God cannot join our soul until we have given our

We must become detached from all our desires and appetites; only then will our arms be free to receive God's embrace.

consent, no more than the lover can be joined to his beloved, however much he loves her, while she still loves others. But God is joined to our soul the very moment our soul loves him. It is an automatic union.

As we cannot pour wine into a jug that is already full unless we first empty it, so the soul cannot be filled by God if it is not first emptied of everything else.

But before receiving God's embrace we must endure the pain of being detached from everything else. We must become detached from all our desires and appetites, from everything we cling to; only then will our arms be free to receive God's embrace.

Love always presses the lover toward union with the beloved, and so God, who loves our soul from all eternity, immediately joins it, without delay, as soon as there is no obstacle in the way.

The process of detachment may take place slowly over a number of years, or it can happen all in a moment. But God bursts in violently the moment the soul is alone. Then the soul is flooded by God, for, as St. John of the Cross says, there is no vacuum in the universe; to empty ourselves of all things means filling ourselves with God. But if the soul has even one single attachment left, one single affection for what is not God, then God cannot enter. For if there is one single affection, the soul will latch onto this, for it must embrace something, and then it will not be fully free for God. First we must go through the agony of possessing no created thing. First we must experience death. Then we fall into God's embrace.

As long as we do not surrender completely to God, neither does God surrender completely to us. The supreme sacrifice is demanded. But the reward is also supreme. We exchange the multitude of particular, finite, and fleeting beauties for absolute, infinite, and eternal beauty.

The journey to God is like an interplanetary flight that becomes more and more difficult the more we try to escape. But once we are out of range of earth's gravity, the journey becomes ever easier, as we are drawn more and more by the gravity of the planet that is our destination.

As long as we do not surrender completely to God, neither does God surrender completely to us.

The starry sky is one great prayer.

The Source

NATURE IS religious in its very essence. The starry sky is one great prayer, and so is every beautiful landscape and the silence of lonely places.

The crickets and the stars speak to us of God, both telling us about their Creator. The whole universe yearns for union with God, the source from whom it came forth. All things are dispersed from their source in God and long to be reunited. The law of love is the supreme physical and biological law of the universe and the one moral law ("A new commandment I give to you: that you should love one another as I have loved you").

All our desires and hungers, whether for food, sex, or friendship, are one single appetite, a single hunger, for union with one another and with the universe. It is a cosmic communion that finds fulfillment only in Christ ("When I am raised on high, I shall draw all things to me"). And when Christ returns to the Father, we all return with him. He described this cosmic return in the parable of the prodigal son.

We have come from God's womb. We are as much part of God as the unborn child belongs to its mother. And we long to return to the maternal womb. Meanwhile our soul cries to God as the calf cries for its mother and as the mother cow calls for her calf.

We are drawn toward God as the moth makes for the flame, as fishes rise to the surface of the water attracted by the fisherman's torch, as the stag is dazzled by the hunter's lamp.

We are born in love, and when we open our eyes we see everywhere the reflection of the One we love, but we do not see him directly. So things drive us mad with love.

All things both charm and disappoint us. They charm us because they are a reflection and image of God. They disappoint us because they are an image but not the reality: they are not God.

There is nothing ugly in the universe. There is only beauty or the relative absence of beauty, the relative absence of the divine reflection in a particular thing.

Beauty, joy, and pleasure are spread through all things. All things are illuminated by beauty to a greater

Our soul cries to God as the calf cries for its mother and as the mother cow calls for her calf.

81

All the beauty we see is like a trickle of water that leads us back to its source.

or lesser degree, as though by a light that is diffused. But God is not spread or diffused; God is the source of light itself.

All things bear an element of beauty, but they are not Beauty itself. God is the light that bathes all beautiful bodies, and in God there is nothing that is not beautiful. This is why, after having tasted God, every other beauty or pleasure becomes insipid and unsatisfying. But every delight leads us to seek God, the source of all delight and all beauty.

All the beauty we see is like a trickle of water that leads us back to its source. What is the marvelous origin of this beauty, where does this being I love come from? How beautiful this source must be!

Children's smiles, flowers, the fish of the sea, the moving stars, all are fleeting beauties that come from God, shine in our sight for a moment, and vanish in the depths of the One who created them. Why do we go on seeking these fleeting beauties and not turn to their inexhaustible source, the hearth from which all these sparks of beauty emerge, sparkle, and then disappear?

All things have their supreme existence in God. Everything that exists has its existence in God. And the reality we see is like a shadow of all that is God. It is as unreal compared to God's reality as a colored photograph compared to the reality it represents.

Butterflies, snow, mountains are all reflections of a divine perfection that exists to the highest degree and, preeminently, in God. In God there is an infinite butterfly, snow, and mountain, and these are the archetypes of those we see here, belonging to God's very essence. The things we see here are limited, finite, contingent, and individual, but in God the butterfly, the snow, and the mountains are one same concentrated infinite thing. The archetypes of the butterfly and the mountain converge in God, because God is infinite and thus everything at once. They are the same simple thing that is God.

God shines in matter, although God is infinitely far from matter, and although matter is opaque and composed of gross atoms. The reflection of God's supreme beauty is what produces other beauties scattered here and there, the blue sea, the seagull, the beauty of human

All things have their supreme existence in God. Everything that exists has its existence in God.

In God, flower, love, poem, and music are one infinite, one pure act.

faces, and of herons, and of quiet green tropical rivers flowing under palms in the evening light.

What will it be like to see this beauty in itself, unveiled, face to face and not reflected in resistant matter but as it is concentrated in God? There you will see the beauty you saw in the sea and in faces and snow and the heron, not scattered in transitory individual reflections, but concentrated in one thing, in one being.

These are the scattered pages of the book of the universe that Dante, in his last canto, says he saw united again into one book by love.

This is the beam of light in which St. Benedict in his ecstasy saw the universe contained.

The plane flying through the sky, the car running along the road, the woods, flowers, children, the divine comedy, everything that exists has an eternal existence in God. But in God they are not separate and individual things as they are in their present reality as creatures. They are one single essence, God's very essence; they are God. Here on earth things exist separately: a flower, a love, a poem, a piece of music. But in God, flower, love, poem, and music are one infinite, one pure act.

The contemplation of God is a recapitulation and synthesis of all creation. But all must die in order to return to their origin, to the unity of all things that is God. And we must renounce everything, including ourselves who are part of this totality, in order to return to the All. Only by dying to ourselves can we find our identity, because our identity is not in ourselves but in the All. Our center is in God who is also the center of all things. And by communicating with all things we also find ourselves, and finding ourselves we are united with all things. To surrender ourselves is to find ourselves, and to lose ourselves is to be saved ("He who saves his life will lose it and he who loses his life for love of me will save it"). We live in a paradoxical universe.

Our self is solitude, and whoever resists suffering and dying, whoever does not want to give but to hang on to the self, remains outside the unity of all things, which is God. ("If the grain of wheat does not die, it remains alone.... ")

The contemplation of God is a recapitulation and synthesis of all creation.

Inner Structures

*Everything in nature has
a trademark,
God's trademark.*

As the soul of the artist is reflected in the work of art, so created things reflect God in their inmost structure. Go into the fields in the early morning and pay attention to the smells, the colors, the birdsongs. In all this there is a reflection of God.

Everything in nature has a trademark, God's trademark: the stripes on a shell and the stripes on a zebra; the grain of the wood and the veins of the dry leaf; the markings on the dragonfly's wings and the pattern of stars on a photographic plate; the panther's coat and the epidermal cells of the lily petal; the structure of atoms and galaxies. All bear God's fingerprints.

There is a style, a divine style in everything that exists, which shows that it was created by the same artist. Everything is multiplicity within unity. Everything is both like other things and unique. Every individual thing has its own manner of being; it is that thing and not anything else. At the same time there are millions and millions of others like it, both minute creatures and

In the image of God who created them, all beings are at once one and many, from the galaxy to the electron.

immense stars. Everything has its own stripes, speckles, spots, dapples, veins, or grain — the caterpillar, the clay pot, the chameleon, the Klee painting and the Persian carpet, sea spray, stalactites, white agate veins in pebbles, the carpet of autumn leaves, wood, marble, sea shells, and the skeleton of the reptile.

They all have God's fingerprints. This is the seal of the Trinity, of God three in one, infinite multiplicity in infinite unity, the unity of what is distinct.

In the image of God who created them, all beings are at once one and many, from the galaxy to the electron.

No two caterpillars are alike, no two atoms, no two stars, even though they look the same in the sky at night. But all things also have something in common. The poet seeks to discover this pattern, this design running throughout creation, and tries to see how even the most different things have an underlying likeness. The mountains skip like rams and the hills like young lambs. ... Your hair is like a flock of goats winding through the mountains of Gilead.

Sin and Freedom

Every work of art gives praise to God.

THE CHORUS of frogs and crickets on moonlit nights, the cries and calls and complaints of all animals, the cock crowing in the distance, the mooing cow, the barking dog, and all other mysterious country sounds are a divine office just like the office chanted by monks. They are psalms in another language. They are prayers.

Songbirds ask the Father for their daily bread and pray that his will be done on earth as it is in heaven. In their own way they bless God's name. So all other animals also pray the Our Father, according to their own manner.

Every work of art gives praise to God. So too do the stars proclaim the glory of God in the heavens. All true art is also a sort of prayer. It does not have to be specifically religious in content to give glory to God, because all true art is fundamentally religious.

God's holiness is manifest everywhere in everything, even in pigs' eyes.

Everything in nature is pure, the spit of a tubercular case as well as the clear water surrounding the islands

An animal or a tree is the exact image of an idea in the mind of God.

in the Caribbean. Worms and herons are equally pure and lovely. All matter is pure and holy because it comes from God's hands. Everything is clean except sin. Everything is pure except our fallen nature. A landscape is pure because it lacks the disordered appetites of fallen humanity. And animals are pure because they are not proud or overbearing. And when a person is a saint, with no disordered appetites, neither proud nor overbearing, that person's rational soul assumes the same purity as woods and lakes, worms and herons.

An animal or a tree is the exact image of an idea in the mind of God. (God's mind is God's essence because everything in God is God's essence.) Each is a faithful message expressing precisely what God wanted to express by it and nothing more. Every material thing is perfectly obedient. Everything faithfully fulfills in its being what God wants it to be. Every star, as the prophet Baruch says, is crying in heaven, "Here I am!" All irrational things are the fulfillment of God's desire.

The human body is also holy and cannot sin. Only our will can sin, and where there is no will there is no sin.

The presence of God in all things means that God is a silent spectator of our sins, and the One who is infinite innocence is forced to become our unwilling accomplice as well as our victim. Thus, sin is added to sin.

To sin is to tyrannize God. But it is also a tyranny imposed on ourselves as well as on God. The damned have committed an enormous injustice against themselves. Sin is not free; it is the surrender of freedom. But it makes us feel we are exercising our freedom, just as dictators, in their propaganda, like to represent themselves as the "people's servants." Many think they are free because they do as they "like," but they do not realize that they are being dictated to from within and that this dictator governs their will and makes them do what they do not want to do. Later, they are repentant, because they have done what they did not want. Nevertheless, they had thought they were free because the dictatorship is internal; it was installed at the very center of their will.

The tyrant is within us, and yet we are his slaves.

To sin is to tyrannize God.

Poverty

ADAM WAS NAKED in Eden. So poverty is the paradisi-
acal state. Adam was as poor as the animals, as poor
as St. Francis, as poor as Christ.

After the fall humans could no longer be naked.
Henceforth a monk's habit is the clothing most like the
nakedness of paradise.

Poverty is also closest to our true condition, while
riches are a disguise. We put on clothes to cover ourselves and to hide our inner nakedness. Falsehood and
riches are synonymous.

Riches are also a falsification of things. A rich dress, a
rich house falsifies the original authenticity of the ma-
terials, they hide the natural nakedness of things, they
perpetrate a fraud.

But there is a splendor in poor things, the splendor of
what is real. A rich thing is always less real than a poor
thing. That is why Thoreau said that it was important for
a man to be able to go out wearing patched trousers. The
splendor of poor things made of clay, straw, homespun,

or plain wood, the coarse, the rough, the crude, the common is the nakedness of matter. It is like the splendor of the naked body. Such things have the same simple splendor as works of art in their texture and color.

If humans had not lost their innocence they could go naked. St. Francis's only possessions were a pair of sandals, a sack, and a rope girdle (and sometimes he even did without them).

The deceitfulness of riches is the confusion between what we have and what we are. We think we are more because we have more. We buy a car and think the car has become part of ourselves, like an extra limb. Thus St. Augustine said that giving up riches hurt like losing a limb. And if people admire our car, we feel that they are admiring us. We think of the things we have as part of ourselves, like a mollusk with a shell that does not belong to it. So the possession of things is a falsification of ourselves.

Rich people think they *are* what they *have.* They show off their things to be admired for them as if they were them. They want to be valued for what they *have* rather than for what they *are.* The Latin poet Propertius saw

The deceitfulness of riches is the confusion between what we have and what we are.

We can possess the universe only by being poor.

the true value of poverty when he boasted he had won the love of a woman by his poems and not by his possessions.

Riches are a deception. Those who think they own a piece of earth on this planet because they have a property deed are as mad as those who have staked claims to a piece of the moon through deeds granted them by some fraudulent agency. A wood or a meadow is owned by the birds and animals that enjoy it, by the loving couple who walk there, or by the hermit who lives there, not by the person who holds the deed. That person possesses only a scrap of official paper disfigured by ugly legal prose.

We own the whole of nature and all the earth and all countries and the starry sky. But we lose all this if we limit our sense of ownership to a few acres of land. We can possess the universe only by being poor, as the birds who are poor possess the sky and the fishes who are poor possess the water and as St. Francis possessed all things. That is why St. Francis called poverty a great treasure ("we are not worthy of so great a treasure!"). He said the greatest luxury was to sit and eat on a beautiful rock by a stream under the blue sky. The poor rich people had to be satisfied with a cramped dining room.

We are children of God, and God is Lord of all. As God's children we too are lords of all the riches in the world. We are surrounded by fabulous riches and we have only to stretch out our hand and take hold of them. A handful of clear water flowing through my fingers is not worth less than a handful of diamonds. We only appreciate it less because it is more abundant. A golden fish in the lake, a jade green frog, a shining pebble, a stick floating in the water, all these are treasures, although no one will put a fictitious money value on them.

Anyone who buys a field and puts a fence round it loses all the rest of nature and everything else. So religious poverty does not mean possessing little but not possessing anything, total dispossession in order to possess everything. We do not limit ourselves to the legal possession of a few things that we claim by virtue of a scrap of paper. For what is more our own than the air, the sun, the earth, the sky, and the sea?

And poverty is also a virtue of the Trinity because God's life is communitarian and communistic, and each

A handful of clear water flowing through my fingers is not worth less than a handful of diamonds.

Only by not coveting, only by giving up everything can we possess everything.

of the three divine persons gives himself totally to the others. In the Trinity there is no "mine" or "thine," even though there is an "I" and a "Thou."

The deceitfulness of riches also lies in thinking that material things can be embraced by something as spiritual as the soul. In Nicaragua we had a dictator who could not satisfy his lust for land. He grabbed more and more land but was never satisfied. Although he held the title deeds the land still did not become his, and however much he grabbed, he remained as poor as he was before, and so he went on wanting more and more. The green fields with their cows and trees and the stream that meandered across them remained as unpossessed as they had been before. He had the title deeds to the land but it was not his. Whoever walked over it and enjoyed the view or fished in the river and then went away without coveting more possessed the land, although they may have been poor persons with no title deeds.

Only by not coveting, only by giving up everything can we possess everything. That is why St. Paul says that those who own something should behave as if they owned nothing, and those who buy anything should behave as if they bought nothing, and those who marry should behave as though they were unmarried.

Money is a tyrant.

Money

MONEY IS A TYRANT, or as Christ said in the language of antiquity, it is a "master" (which for the ancients also meant a god). "No man can serve two masters...." Then he goes on to call money by the name of the god of Sidon, Mammon, for money is also an idol: "You either worship God or Mammon."

On another occasion Christ identifies money with another form of totalitarianism and another god: "Render to Caesar the things that are Caesar's and to God the things that are God's." In saying this he was not legitimizing the things that are Caesar's, as many have thought, nor was he putting two equally legitimate orders side by side: God's and Caesar's. The irony of the phrase is obvious. The money is not Caesar's; it merely

97

Christ is saying that money is not ours but Caesar's and we are God's.

bears his image. Still, Christ says that it is Caesar's because of this. Christ is saying that money is not ours but Caesar's and we are God's. "Render to Caesar the things that are Caesar's" means: Leave the money to Caesar...it is rubbish. "Render to God the things that are God's" means that we should surrender ourselves to God because we are God's and bear God's image.

Money belongs to tyranny, cruelty, pride, and idolatry — in short, to Caesar. All coins and notes bear Caesar's image. (That is why St. Francis forbade his friars to handle money.)

The first of the ten commandments, not to make graven images or worship idols, sounds to us like a commandment for primitive peoples still at the stage of polytheism, an archaeological relic with no relevance to civilized society.

But modern materialism is the same as ancient polytheism, and the world has never had as many idols as it has now. Cars, film stars, political leaders, ideologies — these are modern idols. City streets and highways are full of idols, the idols of commercial and political propaganda, the smiling deities of wealth and abundance, of nutrition and hygiene, the gods of beer and corn flakes and toothpaste, or the faces of dictators and political leaders, the dark divinities of terror and war, destruction and death.

And the same forces of nature worshiped by primitive humanity in the form of fire and thunder are also worshiped by modern humans in the form of electricity and atomic energy.

To possess God means to detach ourselves from things.

Possession

FROM MICROCOSM to macrocosm, all creation speaks of God's infinity. We should see all things as symbols and images, as photographic images of God, rather than as things of intrinsic value, to be possessed and enjoyed as ends in themselves. To possess God means to detach ourselves from things. To detach ourselves from things is to embrace God.

Only God can be truly possessed. If I see a thing

I like and I buy it, I do not thereby possess it. Even though I can give it away or sell it, I have not therefore possessed it. The thing remains inviolate because our faculty of possession lies deep within us, where external things cannot reach. That is why all those who possess things are dissatisfied. This dissatisfaction cannot be cured (only made worse) by possessing yet more things.

There is a sort of invisible glass wall between us and external objects. We dash against it like moths, without ever being able to penetrate it. Outside the window the world goes on smiling at us, untouched, unreached.

And we cannot possess the people we love. They (and we) remain inviolate in their deepest selves. Even between husband and wife there is always a certain distance. They do not become completely one, even though they may wish it. They have only the illusion of union.

Only God can be possessed. God alone can come into our deepest self, and that is where we possess and are possessed. God alone has the key.

God does not come from outside but from inside. God

Only God can be possessed. God alone can come into our deepest self.

We can join God without taking leave of ourselves. Indeed we can join God only by dwelling in the very center of ourselves.

enters our castle by way of secret passages and silent means of communication.

And we can join God without taking leave of ourselves. Indeed we can join God only by dwelling in the very center of ourselves.

Does that mean we can never possess any creatures? This thought might torment us for all eternity, because we would never cease to remember creatures, and we would be tormented by the memory of what we might never possess. Yes, we can possess creatures, but only in God. By possessing God we possess everything, because God possesses all things. All things came from God and will return to God in Jesus. "When I am lifted on high I will draw all things to me," said Christ. And when all things are drawn to him they will also be drawn to me, for he is more me than I am myself; he is my deepest self.

But first we must renounce all things. That is why St. John of the Cross said the way to possess all things is to be dispossessed of all things.

Meanwhile we are like birds shut in a room beating against the glass walls. They see before them a country in lovely light, but they cannot escape. Thus we beat against creatures; we are deceived because we see God through them. But we crash into them because they are solid and do not allow us to pass through to God. Only God's light passes through them. And only by turning aside from this light shining through creatures, only by turning back toward the dark can we find the way out to the garden, to freedom and light, to God.

Only by turning back toward the dark can we find the way out to the garden, to freedom and light, to God.

Appearances

W E CAN WATCH the dance of protons and neutrons forming marvelous shapes before our eyes, like the patterns in a kaleidoscope. But the patterns are illusory; they are no more than colored chips shining for a moment in the light that is God.

The whole world is made of shadows — shadows on the wall of a cave, as Plato said; shadows on a movie or television screen, as we would say.

God, who is hidden in darkness, is the true reality, and God cannot be perceived through the senses, the mind, or the imagination.

Like the movie stars whom we see singing and laughing on a screen, even though they are but images made of light and shade, the stars in the sky shining brightly in the night are also merely shadows. Sometimes we may be looking at stars that no longer exist. They have been dead for millions of years, even though their light still reaches us. They are no more real than the film stars who died long ago, but whom we still see laughing and singing on the screen.

With our eyes, our ears, and our sense of touch, we perceive fleeting images on the screen of our senses. But this is not reality. Death will bring an end to the spectacle and return us to reality. Meanwhile we gape at the world like children staring at television.

God, who is hidden in darkness, is the true reality, and God cannot be perceived through the senses, the mind, or the imagination. We can apprehend God only in the dark light of faith, beyond the senses, the imagination, and the mind. For faith is not really darkness but an invisible light, like an X-ray, which penetrates reality at a greater depth than the light we see.

The Soul

Gᴏᴅ's ᴘʀᴇꜱᴇɴᴄᴇ is invisible and obscure, like the presence of another person that we sense in a darkened room.

We have often felt God's presence within us without realizing it.

We have often felt God's presence within us without realizing it, believing that we were alone. Sometimes it is a feeling of loneliness or fear, a sense of silence, a mysterious love rushing up inside us.

After a party or a dance, when you come home to your room in the small hours and find yourself alone, perhaps in the silence you may feel the presence of another, a sad face that is near you that is not your own. And you feel your own emptiness. You are afraid to look in the mirror, knowing that what you see is not you, that your face is a mask. You are afraid to look at yourself face to face because it is like looking at a corpse. You are afraid to be alone by yourself. It is like the fear you feel in an empty house.

You feel that you — you alone in the universe — are far away from God. The galaxies in the heavens and

We feel the Beloved's presence, like a mysterious caress in the darkness.

the slow geological evolution of the earth, the flora and fauna of the sea as well as the earth — all these obey God's law, and you do not obey.

But this will of God that you do not obey is not something outside you. It is not imposed on your will from the outside. It is more your own than your own will and more you than you are yourself. It is your deepest self and truest identity and the ultimate will of your being.

We feel the Beloved's presence, like a mysterious caress in the darkness. God is present within us, but we do not see him. We see only material reality, a reality as false as technicolor films and the advertisements on television.

Sometimes, even when I was far from God, a faint face would come into my dreams. Sometimes it came to me when I was alone in the silence of the night, after returning from a party. It was the God I had neglected and relegated to the darkness of my unconscious. But God was imprinted on my soul, faint and sorrowful like the face of Christ printed on Veronica's veil. My pain, my dream, my terror in the night was this face on Veronica's veil.

Love is inside us, drawing us to the center of ourselves, the center that is God. For love always seeks union, the identification of the lover and the beloved. There is someone within me who is not me. We are made in such a way that God is the center of our being, so that to turn in on ourselves is to draw near to God. Even though we cannot reach God, because the distance between us is infinite, God is also infinitely close to us, infinitely within.

Love is inside us, drawing us to the center of ourselves, the center that is God.

Images

WE ARE living portraits of God, living works of art. Our deepest mystery, the ultimate secret of our being is that we are not just ourselves; we are images. In our essence we are called not just to be ourselves, but a copy, a photograph of another. Only when we reflect this other are we ourselves. We are a blank screen

We were born of a chaos made fertile by God.

upon which God is projected. If the film is taken away, nothing remains.

This duality is the secret of our being. There is something within us that is the All, and at the same time we are nothing. We are a nothing upon which the All projects itself. But we can blur the image of this All. The soul in a state of sin is the Nothing.

On the one hand we are children of Nothing and on the other hand children of God, because God made us out of nothing. Nothing and God — that is the duality within us.

We came from God, in whom we were from all eternity. We were part of God, and we shall never be satisfied until we return to God. Meanwhile we are in exile. We are persons displaced from God. But it is also true that we came from nothing. For when we were in God we were not ourselves but God; becoming ourselves meant coming out of nothing. We were born of a chaos made fertile by God. This infinite nothing, this chaos from which we come, is what the saints see inside themselves when they also see God, and that is the reason for their terror and humility. They see within themselves this nothing, which is total absence, and lack of everything, the very essence of rot and decay, of autumn, death, and forgetfulness. We are made of this, this aging and autumn, the stuff of death, of corpses; alone we wither and perish.

Hunger and plague and the horrors of war also give us an idea of what we are. For if we destroy the image of God projected onto us, we become the face of melancholy, pain, and death. Beneath every being lies a grinning corpse. In the darkness of our depths we may laugh, but our laugh is the grimace fixed on the faces of the dead in the mortuary freezers. This is what children are afraid of in the dark, and the child that remains within us goes on fearing the darkness of the dream world, the nothingness from which we came and which we are, the dust we came from and to which we shall return. For we are still dust. The life within us is superficial and intermittent. We are dead when we sleep, and even when we are awake we remain asleep or dead to many things. The artist struggles to maintain this life artificially. And the lover tries to safeguard this life from routine and death by means of love. For every-

If we destroy the image of God projected onto us, we become the face of melancholy, pain, and death.

109

God alone is the living God, eternal life, the ever new, the perpetual freshness of the morning.

thing passes and everything must submit at last to the stillness of death. Art too passes and becomes empty. Beauty grows old and fades, and love grows cold. Everything in the universe is subject to the second law of thermodynamics. God alone is the living God, eternal life, the ever new, the perpetual freshness of the morning. For God is the One who is. God does not have life; God is life. "If anyone thirst, let him come to me and drink. He who believes in me, as the Scripture has said, 'out of his heart shall flow rivers of living water'" (John 7:37–38).

God's Will

EVERYTHING THAT HAPPENS is a sacrament of God's will. As the body of Christ is hidden beneath the appearance of bread and wine, so God's will is hidden beneath the appearances, the bread and wine, of day-to-day happenings.

Every historical event is as sacred as the Scriptures, because it is also an expression of the will of God. And the humblest everyday event is also an expression of God's will, and therefore it is as important as the grandest historical event. Missing a train is as important as Napoleon losing the battle of Waterloo.

So there is nothing banal or insignificant in the world ("Every hair on your head is counted"). The most banal event can change the whole history of the world. A falling tile caused the death of a king of Spain. And the child selling newspapers today may merit eight columns tomorrow in every newspaper in the world. But every other banal event also helped shape the history of the world, even if we did not notice it, and the life of every person is equally important, even if it does not make it into the papers.

Our quiet daily life is full of meaning and mystery. It is like a continuation of the hidden years spent by Jesus in Nazareth. Although these years are not described in the Gospels, they are not therefore less important — any more so than the other deeds of Jesus that are not recorded in the Gospels, but that, as St. John says, "were

Every historical event is as sacred as the Scriptures, because it is also an expression of the will of God.

What we call sacred history is only a fragment—inspired by the Holy Spirit—of universal sacred history, the intervention of God's will in the world.

every one of them to be written the world itself could not contain the books that would be written."

What we call sacred history is only a fragment — inspired by the Holy Spirit — of universal sacred history, the intervention of God's will in the world. All history is sacred, and so are the things that happen in our private lives. The Sacred Scriptures from Genesis to Revelation are an illuminated strand running right through human history, from the beginning to the end of the world, from the first day to the last. The rest of the history of the world (and other inhabited worlds if they exist) is not illuminated; it is a plain text. But the will of God is not therefore less present in this text.

This text can be altered by humanity, and humans have altered it a great deal, ever since the first sin. Sacred history is also the history of the will of God, constantly modified by humanity. God decided to bring Israel to the promised land. When the people murmured and wanted to return to Egypt, God changed plans. God decided to exterminate these people and create a new people for Moses. Moses besought God to spare the people of Israel, and God once again apparently changed his mind. God would not exterminate them but neither would they enter the promised land as God had first intended. "Not one shall come into the land where I swore that I would make you dwell" (Num. 14:30).

God's will is an intricate pattern that is constantly being modified by the free will of human beings but is still not destroyed. At each moment God's will is changing to fit circumstances changed by us.

In every particular case God's will takes into account the innumerable consequences that will follow and thus alters all the other cases and circumstances in the universe. When I pray for rain for my harvest or for a stop to the rain so that I can keep an appointment, I am only thinking of the weather from my own point of view. But God thinks of all the effects and consequences of rain or fine weather throughout the world. God's will is the sum of all these things simultaneously taken into account by infinite wisdom and infinite love. So we should gladly accept everything that happens because everything that happens, however unpleasant it appears, is for our good.

The only thing that is not good for us is sin, because

We should gladly accept everything that happens because everything that happens, however unpleasant it appears, is for our good.

The will of God sometimes comes to us in the form of disaster, misery, loneliness, and death.

sin alone depends on us and not on the will of God. Sin is against the will of God; it is our enemy.

But everything that does not depend on our will is the will of God. Even the effects and consequences of sin are the will of God, although the sin itself was our will, and the effects and consequences of the sins of others are also the will of God. One man fires a gun at another man by his own will, but whether the man's revolver is loaded, whether the bullet comes out, the path that the bullet takes, whether the bullet hits its mark, and all the other consequences of this man's action depend on the will of God. So we should bless everything that happens, for all things, even the effects of sin, are the will of God, and the only exception is our consent to sin.

Sometimes we do not want to recognize the will of God because it comes to us in hideous disguise, as when Pilate presented Jesus to the crowd wearing a crown of thorns. Some preferred the dictatorship of Tiberius: "We have no king but Caesar!" The will of God sometimes comes to us in the form of disaster, misery, loneliness, and death. And we prefer Tiberius who is power, pleasure, money, cruelty, and glory. And we cry: "Crucify him! We have no king but Caesar!"

The will of God can appear in the form of cancer or a road accident or the police of a totalitarian state arresting you in the night, and it is difficult to recognize and bless God in these disguises. But all that we call reality is the incarnation of the word of God, what God wishes. All reality is sacred. A chance meeting in the street, missing a train or airplane, they are all the will of God.

God is present not only in the bread and wine of the Eucharist but also in some way in every grain of wheat, and in all wine, water, and oil, and in all reality. God is silently and humbly present in reality, because all reality is a sacrament.

We do not know what is good for us, and we should not desire anything except what God wants or does not want for us. We should accept things as God sends them, because God knows what is good for us. Things happen all round us that we do not understand. Where they come from or where they are going we do not know. We are like a small child at a large airport full of planes

God is silently and humbly present in reality, because all reality is a sacrament.

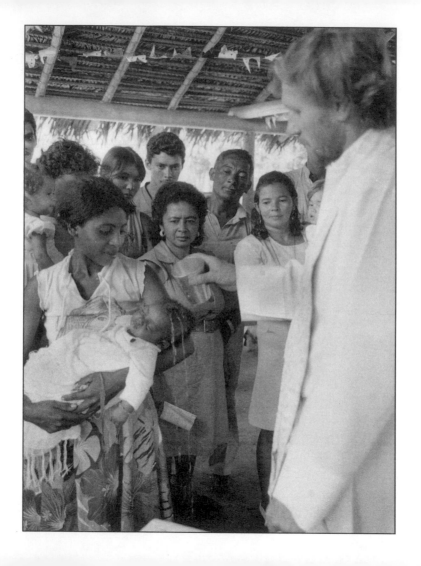

arriving and leaving, and the child cannot get on the plane she wants because she does not know where any of them are going and does not know her own destination. She has to wait to be told which plane she is meant to get on. So we do not know our destination, nor what is good for us, which things that happen do us good or evil, because we do not know the future (and we know the past and the present only in a very partial way).

But sin is believing that we know better than God what is good for us, that God is mistaken on some particular point about us, that what God wants for us in this particular case is wrong for us.

Only God knows what is good for us, because everything that happens and will happen has already happened in God's mind for all eternity, like a photograph taken long ago that we now see for the first time in the darkroom, or like a film already made but that we now see on the screen, or like the light given out by a star millions of years ago but that only now reaches our retina.

God knows that what does not suit me today may suit me tomorrow. And God may want something now that

Sin is believing that we know better than God what is good for us.

Without realizing it, we live surrounded by miracles.

he does not want later, or want something here that he does not want somewhere else, or want something for me that he does not want for others. When they asked St. Joan of Arc at her trial whether God loved the English, she replied: "God does not love the English in France." And this is the mystery of our vocation. God also loves the man who is dictator of Nicaragua, but he does not want him to be the dictator of Nicaragua.

Miracles

WITHOUT REALIZING IT, we live surrounded by miracles. These are not only miracles in the conventional sense, but also what we might call natural miracles. No one loves nature more than God, the Creator of nature, and God wishes his miracles to be ordinary. As the cause of all causes, God prefers that all things have a cause and that causes have their effects and that it all happens in accordance with the laws of nature.

Everything that happens has a meaning, and the ordinary is as meaningful as the miracle. A mouse is a miracle, as Walt Whitman says. Everything ordinary is a miracle, all the more marvelous because we do not pay attention to it. It is the humble unseen miracle of every day.

That is why St. Augustine said that the miracle of the multiplication of the loaves was no greater than the miracle that happens every day in every seed. It was only less "usual."

Creation was not an isolated act by God, remote in time. It is a perennial act that is happening before our eyes at every moment, and also before the eyes of unbelievers, although they still do not believe. We are being created at every moment, brought out of nothing all the time. The whole universe is a perpetual miracle, and the most ordinary everyday events are as miraculous as the miracles at Lourdes.

The ordinary is precisely God's way of working miracles. What we call ordinary is as miraculous as the extraordinary, though we do not see it thus because we are used to it. But for those who live in contact with

We are being created at every moment, brought out of nothing all the time.

God can work miracles by means of coincidence.

God, all life is extraordinary and supernatural and full of miracles.

God works visible miracles to show the world, but within the soul God does not need to work miracles of that kind. God works them through coincidence and everyday events, which are no less miraculous for lack of ostentation.

Sometimes it is difficult for us to tell the difference between a miracle and a coincidence. This is because a coincidence can also be a miracle; God can work miracles by means of coincidence.

In fact nothing happens by chance. What we call chance is really another name for the will of God. Sometimes it is difficult for us to recognize the will of God because it is incarnate in reality, in the natural laws of history, physical phenomena, accidents, chance, luck, coincidence. All this is God's providence.

We usually call only the extraordinary happenings in our life providential and only those things that suit us or that we think suit us. We think it providential if we escape unharmed from a road accident, or if we did not take the plane that crashed. We do not realize that being killed in a road accident or being on the plane that crashes is also providential. Fundamentally this is a residual dualism, a belief that there are two gods, good and evil, and that providence is the victory of the good God over the god of catastrophe and chaos. But there is only one God, and nothing in the universe, save for sin, escapes God's providence. Everything that happens is providential, and everything, save sin, that happens is for our good. Only sin is not providential, because it is the one thing that is not made by God but by human will. Even so, the effects and consequences of sin, which do not depend on humans but on God, are providential. Providence pertains to what is unfavorable as well as the favorable, the ordinary as well as the extraordinary, what does not happen as well as what does happen.

We often do not recognize providence because our will intervenes and resists the will of God, and so we resist providence. But if we attach our will to the will of God and do not do the slightest thing against God's plans, then we see divine providence acting in our lives in the most marvelous way, and chance and the unex-

There is only one God, and nothing in the universe, save for sin, escapes God's providence.

When we say "Our Father," in a spirit of faith and love, we are at home, even in the vast spaces between the stars and the galaxies.

pected and all our daily lives are full of meaning; all our life is full of the most amazing coincidences and miracles.

If you never impose your will in anything but only follow the will of God, then every meeting in the street, every telephone call, every letter you receive will be full of meaning and you will find it makes sense and that it follows a providential plan.

Most people feel themselves alone and unprotected in the universe, as if their only providence were themselves, as if they had been created by themselves or by chance and live in a universe ruled by chance. They feel poor and helpless in a hostile world, like children lost in a wood, and not like beings created by God and placed by God in a benevolent universe also created for our benefit. We are not alone; the One who created us dwells within us and surrounds us. When we say "Our Father," in a spirit of faith and love, we are at home, even in the vast spaces between the stars and the galaxies.

When we realize that the One who governs the course of the stars, the galaxies, and the expansion of the universe is also the One who controls the circulation of our blood and our metabolism and our lowliest daily doings, then we shall feel secure and confident and calm. God takes care of the glowworm as well as the galaxies, and not an atom moves without God's consent. So what in the universe shall we fear?

The physical laws of the universe and the moral law are all one law. Only the moral law is a law of God that can be broken by human beings. We cannot break the laws of God's creation in thermodynamics, for example, but we can break the moral law. We are the only part of the universe that can disobey. And when we obey the will of God we are in harmony with all the rest of the universe, because we are obeying the same law that all physical nature obeys. All non-human creatures obey their creator, as Baruch says: "He that sends forth light, and it goes, calls it again and it obeys him with fear. The stars shine in their watches and rejoice. When he calls them, they say, 'Here we are'; and so with cheerfulness they show light unto him that made them" (Bar. 3:33–35).

Joy can also be a perfect prayer, because it is an act of

We are the only part of the universe that can disobey.

123

Sin is becoming a law to ourselves and abandoning the law of God.

confidence in God, and the certainty that nothing evil can happen to us in the universe. And joy can sometimes also be heroic.

Damnation

S IN IS THE DESIRE to be like gods, that is, the desire to be the center of the universe and to be our own lawgiver.

Sin is becoming a law to ourselves and abandoning the law of God. Sin is tyranny, becoming a dictator over oneself. Those who are damned have been unjust to themselves because they have condemned their own innocent being to be deprived of God eternally, to be nothing.

God abhors the damned because God loves them, and the damned are their own enemy. God loves what they are or should be, what they ought to be in themselves, but now they have become a negation of themselves, an anti-being; because sin is the negation of God and the desire to set oneself up as an anti-God.

Sin is something that is not; it is something that anti-exists. It is full of emptiness. It is something worse than nothing, because nothingness does not exist; it is nothing. But sin is a real nothingness, a living death. The damned person lives in an eternal state of death and is condemned to be eternally nothing.

If God is infinite beauty and goodness, non-God is an infinite horror.

Physical death is merely the transformation of matter, but eternal death is matter in an eternal corpse-like state. It is a sort of counter-matter, an anti-universe, an anti-creation. Eternal death is the horrible grimace of part of the universe turned into a corpse.

The soul in sin is like an extinct star, the horror of a vast, cold, and empty universe where there is no company. God is infinitely good and infinitely beautiful, and so sin is the absence of God, the infinite absence of the good and the beautiful, and thus the presence of the infinitely horrible. If God is infinite beauty and goodness, non-God is an infinite horror. And if God is absolute being, sin, which is the negation of God, is absolute non-being, total emptiness, and most hideous nothingness.

Heaven is the communion of saints, and hell is isolation and loneliness.

The soul is a being and it cannot stop being, but the soul in sin and empty of God is an absolutely cold and empty being; it is totally desolate and full of nothingness.

And the fire of hell is also the fire of love. Hell is a work of divine love, says Dante, because in hell there is also love; but love without hope. Heaven is requited love, love in possession, while hell is disappointed love. The Song of Songs says that jealousy is like the pain of hell; the pain of hell is jealousy. It is loving and being rejected by what you love, it is rejecting love. Anyone who has experienced disappointed love has experienced some of the pain of hell here on earth. Heaven is the communion of saints, and hell is isolation and loneliness. Ontological solitude. The fire of hell is the same fire of concupiscence that sometimes burns in our flesh here on earth. It is selfish love and the burning of unsatisfied desire, of loneliness, and of jealousy. Hell has a "material" fire, and we do not know what this fire is like. But in this atomic age we have learned a little more about the nature of fire. Eternal fire must be an eternal state of molecular or nuclear disintegration of matter. God is love and union, and God's love is the force of molecular cohesion in matter, while hell is eternal disintegration, matter falling apart, at war with itself, and the pain of not loving.

Physical death is merely the beginning of eternal life, "the condition of resurrection," as St. Athanasius says.

Death

D EATH NO LONGER exists for us. Our death occurred in our baptism, through which we shared in the death of Christ; we have died with Christ. Christ died for us and instead of us, and now we need not die. Physical death is merely the beginning of eternal life, "the condition of resurrection," as St. Athanasius says. We who have been baptized have passed through death. Our physical "death" is not a real death, but the passage to our meeting Christ.

Christ is "the first-born of the dead," as St. Paul says. This means Christ was the first (the first-born) to rise again, the first who passed from the womb of death out to the new life, and all those who follow him are

We were not born to die, but to live, to live eternally.

like other children, brothers and sisters from the same mother's womb.

For a monk, death no longer exists. Death has already been overcome. Those who live in union with God fear nothing. No harm can come to them. While the world is chiefly concerned with the brevity of life, for us the shortness of time and the swift passage of the days is our chief joy. We see time pass like an express train, and we feel the excitement of those who are travelling by train to a longed-for destination, a happy meeting. Time is the train speeding to its destination, a train taking us to meet God.

It is not true that life is short. Our life is not short; it is eternal. We do not have death before us, but eternity. We were not born to die, but to live, to live eternally. We do not grieve that time passes so quickly, because it is not life that passes; it is only time (which is, so to speak, the constant passing of that which is not yet into that which is no longer). What lies ahead is eternity, the everlasting present, without future or past, without end, life in an eternal present, eternal life. We do not fear death because we are not going to die; rather, we shall pass on to a more perfect life, more real, more vital, more *alive.*

We resemble the caterpillar that falls asleep in its chrysalis and is changed into a butterfly.

"I saw a new heaven and a new earth," says St. John in the Book of Revelation. The cosmos will not perish; there will not be an "end" of the world, but rather a total renewal. When we read in Scripture that the "stars will fall from the heavens," this means that there will be a new cosmos, a universe with a new structure. And there will be a new life in this new world.

We belong to this new cosmos that is already beginning and whose first seed is the risen body of Christ ("the first-born of the dead" and the "first fruits of the resurrection"). And this seed will grow and multiply till it replaces the old creation ("the kingdom of heaven is like a grain of mustard seed..."). Matter will be organized anew in a "noncorruptible" form, with a new nuclear and cellular structure, and the center of this new cosmos will be the body of Christ, and all creation will revolve round him as the earth and the planets revolve round the sun. "And the city has no need of sun or moon

We belong to this new cosmos that is already beginning and whose first seed is the risen body of Christ.

129

When we take communion with Christ we commune with the resurrection and the renewal of the cosmos.

to shine upon it, for the glory of God is its light, and its lamp is the lamb" (Rev. 21:23). When we take communion with Christ we commune with the resurrection and the renewal of the cosmos ("I am the resurrection and the life"); we drink at the very spring of life.

The cicadas that stay buried in the earth for seventeen years in a larval state and come to life in spring are a symbol of the resurrection of Christ and of our resurrection. Every spring is a symbol of this resurrection.

Life

THE CHRISTIAN LIVES like a traveler, says St. Clement of Alexandria. We are like tourists who leave a country without great regret because we are going home. We do not leave the world sadly, as if we were going into exile, but gladly like exiles returning home, like displaced persons returning to their homeland.

For those who do not live in hope of heaven the pleasures and joys of life are sad because they come to an end. Those who live in hope of heaven are the only ones who can fully enjoy the joys of earth, because they see them as a foretaste of the joys to come. They are glad that earthly joys pass and quickly come to an end because they long for the joys to come.

Now we see as in a glass, says St. Paul, but then we shall see face to face and we shall know as we are known. Now we cannot see things in their mysterious essence, as they are known by God, as they are possessed by God, as they really are. We only see their images that come to us through our senses, a shape, a color, a smell, a feeling, but not the things themselves. They are merely sense images reflected in our brain. We see "as in a glass." But when we see "face to face" everything will be transformed, our friends, everything around us, the whole world. We shall see them for the first time, not through sense images, but in the splendor of what they are. We shall know them as they are known by God (because knowing is loving and loving is knowing) and as we ourselves are known and loved by God. And we shall know God as we are known by God, because we shall also see

Those who live in hope of heaven are the only ones who can fully enjoy the joys of earth.

God "face to face," and not, as we see God now "in a glass," reflected in material things. And when we see God face to face, we shall see all things face to face, as they are seen by God, as they are in God, as they really are.

We shall see beauty face to face, not the beauty shining through things, but beauty in itself. We shall see it directly, not mediated by things; we shall see beauty itself, not beautiful things, we shall see without veils; we shall simply see. Heaven is both unending seeing and unending loving. There, to love is also to see, to possess, to enjoy. We have tasted joys here on earth, some greater than others, and all these joys are the joy of possessing a thing; but things are limited, and so are their joys. The joy of possessing God, however, is like an immense sea of joy, boundless, bottomless, a joy growing ever greater beyond our utmost capacity for joy.

We shall know as we are known. We shall possess God as we are possessed by God; we shall be owners of God as God is our owner; we shall enjoy God as God enjoys; we shall be partakers of the Godhead. For seeing God is possessing God, and possessing God is being like unto

When we see God face to face, we shall see all things face to face, as they are seen by God, as they are in God, as they really are.

133

Only in heaven shall we truly communicate with one another, only in heaven can we speak our most intimate word.

God. "We shall be like him because we shall see him as he is" (1 John 3:2).

And then we shall know each other for the first time, and heaven will be a communion of love. Because here on earth we cannot know each other well. We only know by appearances, and even those who know and love each other best are always a profound mystery to one another, always fundamentally unknown, just as we remain unknown and a mystery to ourselves. Only in heaven shall we truly communicate with one another, only in heaven can we speak our most intimate word, and we shall have no need of language because we shall have a perfect communion of love. Time will be over, says the Book of Revelation. There will no longer be the torment of time passing, of the party ending, and we shall no longer know each other piecemeal as we know each other now, in the constant flow of the river of time. We shall know each other completely, living in the total presence of those we love.

The things we say now are blown away on the wind, smiles fade, and the joy of being with the person we love does not endure. It blows away with time like smoke on the wind. But in heaven there will be neither space nor time. We shall love in eternity, in eternal life, life that is movement, but movement that does not pass away, eternal presence. And there will no longer be the torment of space. Now we can never be with all the people we like at the same time. To be with some we must be absent from others, and there are so many others whom we do not even know, whom we might also like, just as those we now like and are friends with were once unknown and strangers to us. But in heaven we shall all be together, and we shall enjoy the company of all those we now partly know and love and all those others we do not love because we do not know them. Then we shall be close to all humanity, and how great the love will be between those who now love each other here in the changes and chances of space and time, who are close to one another. We shall see again those who have died, those we saw grow old and die, and those who grew old with us. We shall see them all again and no body on earth is as beautiful as their bodies will be then.

The beauty of the human body can give us an idea of what the splendor of the resurrection will be, of what

The beauty of the human body can give us an idea of what the splendor of the resurrection will be.

Touching a human body is a bit like touching heaven.

heaven will be. As Novalis said, touching a human body is a bit like touching heaven. But beauty grows old. And, as St. Paul says, this beauty is to the risen body as the seed is to the plant (1 Cor. 15:35–50). So what can money, success, or pleasure matter to us, when we think of heaven? We no longer fear death; we desire it. We do not grieve for the death of others; we envy them, because we want to get to heaven as quickly as possible. It does not sadden us to grow old. We want to die soon or grow old soon. We want life to fly past (and indeed it does) and for space and time to pass quickly, along with every finite pleasure, every absence, disappointment, pain, disaster, sickness, death, and fear of dying.

Paradise

GOD SET AN ANGEL with a fiery sword at the gate of paradise, and ever since there have been sadness and boredom in every pleasure.

Ever since human beings were expelled from paradise,

they have been trying to get back. Childhood, spring, the discovery of love are all like the remnants of paradise. And there remains the innocence of animals, an innocence that they never lost.

But paradise is not to be found in the tropics, as Columbus believed. It is not to be found in the "tropical paradises" advertised by travel agencies. It is not to be found at Miami Beach. Paradise is on Calvary. "Today you will be with me in paradise." The Good Thief had spoken to Christ of his kingdom. "Remember me when you come into your kingdom." Christ answered him with the word "paradise": "Today you will be with me in paradise." He meant that he was reopening the gates of paradise for us.

This was not a metaphor. As he was dying on the cross and talking to another dying man, it was not the right moment for metaphors. Those who have accepted the cross and gone up Mount Calvary know quite well that this is no place for metaphors.

From the time of Christ's agony and death, paradise has been open to us again. But paradise is found only on Calvary. Paradise is union with God.

Paradise is found only on Calvary. Paradise is union with God.

Those who live in union with God know that no creature has power to harm them.

Union with God makes the earth a paradise once more. Where God is with me, there is paradise and the whole of nature is the lovely background to our friendship, the starry sky, mountains, the apple tree in blossom.

Nature is no longer hostile to those who live in the presence of God. Then they feel safe from all harm, just as Adam did in paradise. Without God's presence we feel danger all round us, a danger that at any time things can wound, crush, suffocate, mutilate, batter, or bite us. But those who live in union with God know that a leaf does not fall without God's consent and that every hair of their head is counted, that no creature has power to harm them.

For those who live in union with God all things are transfigured by a special light, and joy springs from them—even the most common everyday things. Blessedness falls on every moment of their life and there is a kind of enchantment upon everything they touch, everything they do. As Christ said to the woman at the well, the water that I shall give will become a spring of water welling up to eternal life. ("And the woman said to him, 'Sir, give me this water, that I may not thirst, nor come here to draw.' ")

Paradise is love. All lovers feel that they have spent a little time in paradise, but they who live in the love of God live in paradise all the time.

Every human love is a glimpse of eternity. But it is a fleeting glimpse. In this moment we catch a faint glimmer of God's life, which is an eternal motion, an infinite present that never passes away. Human love is a brief eternity, but the joy of God is an eternal movement, because God's eternity is not static but eternal life. God is the source of life, and life is movement.

Every human love is a glimpse of eternity.

Human love took over the language of mystical love, according to Henri Bergson, and not mystical love the language of human love.

In modern times marriage is regarded as a kind of mystical union. Commercial propaganda shows domestic life as a kind of paradise on earth. The husband or wife is expected to be a god or a goddess, which is why there is so much frustration in so many marriages today. Creatures are required to give what only God can give. Both the spouse and the home are expected to satisfy an infinite thirst for love that only God can satisfy.

We feel that if we live an "obscure" life, unknown to the world, it is as if we do not exist.

Knowing and Being Known

WE WANT to be known. Ants happily pass their days climbing up and down a blade of grass, quite content with the tiny corner of creation God has allotted them. They do not want to be well known or famous. They are content to be the anonymous creatures God created, content just to be. They are known by God and that is enough. But we feel that if we live an "obscure" life, unknown to the world, it is as if we do not exist.

The spider spinning its web does not want publicity. The small insect does not sign its autograph, yet even a film star in all her finery is not clothed so gloriously. The cardinal flies swiftly through the wood shunning all publicity. It tries to conceal and not show off its beauty. And the rabbit runs through the wood and hides, content with its hidden life. But we do not want an "obscure" life. We want to be known.

No doubt to be known is to be, and that is why we want to be known (and if we are unknown we feel like shadows). Eternal glory is called glory because it is like human glory; it means being known. But human glory is a false glory, because it means being known by people who are not any more than we are and whose knowledge of us does not affect our being. We are no less if we lead an obscure life unknown to the world. We are no more if we are famous, if our names appear in newspaper headlines and we are interviewed on radio and television.

Our true existence lies in being known by God. We are to the extent that we are known by God. Not being known by God is not being, because God knows everything. The exception is evil, which God does not know, being infinitely innocent.

That is why St. Francis of Assisi so often repeated: "I am what I am before God." And Christ says that God rejects those whom he does not admit to the kingdom of heaven with the words: "I do not know you."

Our true existence lies in being known by God.

141

We are shadows of shadows. That is why human glory is but a shadow.

Our desire for fame comes from our vague realization that we do not fully exist if we do not exist in the mind of Someone outside ourselves. And we feel that being unknown is like not being. But fame does not make us immortal, for the famous ones too are mortal and need to be in the mind of others in order to be. Otherwise they too are shadows. Our reality thus depends on other shadows, and we think we are real because we are reflected in the unreality of others. We are shadows of shadows. That is why human glory is but a shadow.

But heaven also means knowing. "I shall know as I am known," says St. Paul. Heaven is seeing. It is contemplation and vision. Our reward will be seeing, says St. Augustine, because seeing and understanding and grasping are possessing ("knowing," in the biblical sense) and also loving. Seeing is receiving, and just as through our sight and our other senses we receive the perceptible reality around us, so seeing God is receiving God and possessing God. And seeing God is also being like God. "We shall be like him because we shall see him as he is" (1 John 3:2).

Contemplating God is being like God because we are

natural imitators, and to see God is to imitate God. We become more and more like God throughout eternity. That is why a soul that sees God is like unto God.

The soul is essentially a mirror, and so not something valuable in itself (just as the mirror in itself is just glass), but for the beauty reflected in it. The soul's beauty is the beauty of God reflected in it. And the soul without God is a mirror with nothing reflected in it. It is a thing that is not.

Humanity by nature is athirst for knowledge, understanding, and possession. Ultimately this thirst is for God.

To know God is what we seek in journeys, in science, in books, in love. This is why we thirst for experience and our thirst can only be satisfied by God. St. Thérèse of Lisieux looked forward to heaven, thinking that there she would understand how birds and flowers and the wind are made.

But then we shall not know reality in a limited way, through our five senses, as we do now. We shall know total reality, as it is, with a direct knowledge, with the knowledge —in the biblical sense —of loving possession.

The soul's beauty is the beauty of God reflected in it.

Or, as César Vallejo said: "The kisses will be given that you could not give."

Plants and animals are part of our humanity and are called to share with us in the resurrection.

Evolution

BEES GIVE US honey and silk worms clothe us, but the chief service done by plants and animals to human beings is not that they feed and clothe us, not that they serve other animals that in turn serve us, but that they passed life along to us, that they are our forerunners in the long process of evolution. They are part of our humanity and are called to share with us in the resurrection. The fossilized trilobite that lived five hundred million years ago did not die altogether but passed on life to our bodies; in a way it is still living in our bodies and awaiting the resurrection with us.

We are organically connected with all creation, and when Adam sinned, the whole of nature was cursed because of him. "Cursed be the earth because of you," God told him. And at the flood God did not repent only of having made human beings but also all creation. "I will blot out man whom I have created from the face of the ground, man and beast and creeping things, and birds of the air." Because through man "the earth was filled with violence" and "all flesh had corrupted their way upon the earth." Likewise, God's rainbow covenant with Noah after the flood was also a covenant with all creation. "This is the sign of the covenant which I make between me and you and every living creature that is with you." And in the same way Christ's new covenant is not only with humanity but with all creatures. And when Christ rose from the dead he told his apostles to preach the gospel to every creature (not humans alone). And so all creatures groan with us as if in labor, in expectation of the resurrection.

Because all creatures on earth are related through biological evolution, the resurrection of the body is but one further stage, indeed the final stage. With the resurrection of Christ this final stage has already begun. Christ is the first specimen of this new "biological" era or, as St. Paul said, "the first-born" and the "first

Christ's new covenant is not only with humanity but with all creatures.

145

Every birth is painful, for every birth is also a death.

fruits of the resurrection." Our resurrection is like one more metamorphosis, and we can better imagine this by considering the sequence of living things through the pre-Cambrian, the Cambrian, the Silurian, the Devonian, the Paleozoic, and the Mesozoic periods. St. Paul said as much when he said we have only to consider the metamorphosis of a grain of wheat.

Every birth is painful, for every birth is also a death. When we came forth from our mother's womb as infants, it meant the death of our former life, the end of our comfortable fetal existence. For that reason we are born crying. And all the other stages of growth are further painful deaths that each of us must suffer. "Unless a grain of wheat falls into the earth and dies, it remains alone, but if it dies it bears much fruit" (John 12:24). And unless the cell subdivides it remains alone, but if it subdivides it bears much fruit. And the stars too are like grains of wheat. They too are born through painful deaths. They are produced by great explosions.

The whole cosmos is like a great grain of wheat. And like the child in its mother's womb, it is waiting to be born. It groans with labor pains.

This new birth is also painful, and we resist it because we are very comfortable as we are, enclosed in our present cosmos. It is like the warm darkness of our mother's womb, where it is better to say we sleep than that we live. We do not want to be born and to go out into life. But the life process must go on and we must go on to the new life or die. As Jesus said to Nicodemus: "Unless a man is born again he cannot enter the kingdom of God."

Christ is the first-born ("the first-born of the dead"). The empty tomb on the morning of the resurrection was like a womb newly delivered of its first child. Some of the matter of which we are made (calcium, iron, phosphorus, potassium) has left our universe and now belongs to a new creation. There has been an empty space in the matter of the universe ever since the tomb was found empty on the morning of the resurrection. Or as the proper for the Ascension says, "Set at the right hand of thy glory the substance of our frail human nature." Frail human biology was seated at God's right hand — and we too as sharers in that biology.

We do not want to be born and to go out into life. But the life process must go on and we must go on to the new life or die.

It is a natural biological process, as the parable clearly indicates: "And he said: 'The kingdom of God is as if a man should scatter seed upon the ground, and should sleep and rise night and day, and the seed should sprout and grow, he knows not how. The earth produces of itself, first the blade, then the ear, then the full grain in the ear. But when the grain is ripe, at once he puts in the sickle because the harvest has come'" (Mark 4:26–29).

And the harvest will come sooner than we think. The prophet Amos says that in those days those who are still plowing will see the reaper right behind them.

The harvest will come sooner than we think.

The Mustard Seed

IN MANY PARABLES Christ told us that the kingdom of heaven is an evolutionary process. It is a grain of wheat, a seed that the sower goes out to sow, a leaven that a woman puts in a lump of dough, a grain of mus-

The kingdom of heaven is a slow process, as slow as the formation of the stars over billions of years.

tard seed that, when it is sown, is the smallest of all seeds but when it grows becomes one of the largest shrubs, permitting the birds of the air to find shelter in its branches. He used similes from nature and ordinary life to tell us that the kingdom of heaven belongs to the same process as nature and ordinary life. And at the same time he wanted to tell us that the kingdom of heaven is a slow process, as slow as the formation of the stars over billions of years, as slow as the formation of the earth through long geological ages. And all that time the kingdom of heaven was already beginning to be formed on earth — as unnoticed as the growing mustard seed or the grain of wheat.

The cosmos is made not only of space but also of time. If we lift our eyes to the stars we see them not only through space but also through time. And if we look with a telescope at the furthest stars, our telescope takes us not only through space but also through time, allowing us to see something that existed aeons ago.

This time dimension, which we find in all the universe, is also like a parable of the kingdom of heaven. "If you had as much faith as a grain of mustard seed...."

And we know that the mustard seed contains locked up and folded within it the mustard bush, and that all biological evolution was contained in the first cell. We have the seeds. They do not look like much. But faith takes a handful of very ugly, wrinkled, dried out seeds....

And there is a hidden mystery in these parables about seeds: seeds belong to evolution. We are descended from them, or rather we are the final development of these same seeds, and together with all the other beings in the animal and vegetable kingdom we form the tree of life. The kingdom of heaven is not only like a seed; it *is* a seed. And just as the grain of wheat and the mustard seed and the cell must divide in order to reproduce, so too must a person die in order to grow, to form the complete human being, or the mystical body, the fullness of the stature of the body of Christ, according to St. Paul. Within this mystical body, our genealogical tree, all living beings are contained, just as the birds of heaven find shelter in the branches of the mustard tree. For the kingdom of heaven is in the process of evolution. It is a biological continuation of the kingdom of min-

The kingdom of heaven is in the process of evolution.

The kingdom of heaven is social, an ecclesia, a community, a kind of spiritual communism.

erals, vegetables, animals, and also of human kingdoms, of human socialization or hominization, as Teilhard de Chardin says.

The Jews expected the kingdom of God to be an earthly kingdom, and in this they were not mistaken, for the kingdom of heaven is also an earthly kingdom. It is the heavenly kingdom established on earth, and that is why we pray for it to come to us in the Our Father. The kingdom of heaven is a kingdom — or as we might say today, a republic — that is, a social order. The kingdom of heaven is social, an *ecclesia,* a community, a kind of spiritual communism. But the Jews (like Marxists today) were mistaken in thinking it was a social order like those already existing on earth. As Christ said to Pilate, his kingdom is not of this world; it is of a different order. So Christ said to his apostles: "The kings of the Gentiles exercise lordship over them; and those in authority over them are called benefactors. But not so with you; rather let the greatest among you become as the youngest, and the leader as one who serves" (Luke 22:25–26). That is to say, the order is reversed. It is a kingdom without subjects, a democratic kingdom, a nation of kings, as St. Peter says (1 Pet. 2:9). Isaiah had prophesied the coming of this kingdom as a new social order that would be realized here on earth: "The wolf shall dwell with the lamb and the leopard shall lie down with the kid, and the calf and the lion and the fatling together, and a little child shall lead them. The cow and the bear shall feed; their young shall lie down together; and the lion shall eat straw like the ox. The sucking child shall play over the hole of the asp, and the weaned child shall put his hand into the adder's den" (Isa. 11:6–8).

Christ came to earth to establish this kingdom. It is already established in a small way, in religious communities, in monasteries, under artificial conditions as in a laboratory. Monasteries are trying out the social system of the future. But Christ did not come to establish his kingdom only in the laboratory, in monasteries. He came to make his kingdom the social reality of villages, of nations, of humanity. The church is humanity. And the present church is the small, seemingly insignificant seed of this humanity. That is why the kingdom of heaven is like a grain of mustard seed.

The church is humanity. And the present church is the small, seemingly insignificant seed of this humanity.

The human spirit is much greater than these universes, because we can look at these worlds and understand them and be aware of them, but they cannot understand us.

The Universe

O UR GALAXY HAS three hundred thousand million stars, some with the brightness of three hundred thousand suns, with a hundred million galaxies in the universe to be explored. But when you look at the universe on a starry night, you should not feel your littleness and insignificance but rather your greatness. The human spirit is much greater than these universes, because we can look at these worlds and understand them and be aware of them, but they cannot understand us. These worlds are made up of simple molecules, like the hydrogen molecule that has just one nucleus and one electron. But the human body is made of more complicated molecules and also has life that is of a complexity far beyond the molecular world. We also have consciousness and love. And when a lover says that the eyes of his beloved are brighter than stars, this is no exaggeration (even though the star Sigma of the Dorado is three hundred thousand times brighter than the sun) because the light of intelligence and love shines in her eyes and not in Sigma of the Dorado, Alpha of the Lyra, or Antares. And even were the radius of the universe a hundred thousand million light years, the radius of the universe is still limited. And the humblest of human beings is greater than the whole material universe. Human greatness is of an order beyond mere size, for the whole material universe can be contained as a small point in the human mind that is thinking of it.

And these worlds are dumb. They praise God, but with unconscious praise. They do not know they are doing it, whereas we are the voice of these worlds and their awareness. These worlds are not capable of love, whereas we are.

Our mind, however, is not separate from these worlds. We are also this vast universe, its conscience and its heart. We are the vast universe that thinks and loves.

According to Plato, the human soul completes the universe. It was created so that the cosmos might have a mind. Humanity is the perfection of the visible creation and we cannot think ourselves low and vile ("vile worm of the earth"), for this would mean calling all God's work low and vile.

We are also this vast universe, its conscience and its heart.

We are the mind of the cosmos.

And the vastness of the universe you see on a starry night becomes even greater if you think of yourself too as part of this same universe, and realize that you are the universe itself in self-awareness, and that in addition to its dimensions of time and space it has, in you, a further dimension that is even greater.

We are the mind of the cosmos. And the incarnation of the Word in a human body means his incarnation into the whole cosmos.

For the whole cosmos is in communion. The calcium that is in our bodies is the same calcium that is in the sea (and we took it from the sea because our life came from the sea). And the calcium of our bodies and of the sea is the same as the calcium of the sky, the stars' calcium and the calcium floating in the interstellar oceans from which the stars came (for the stars are a concentration of the thin matter in the interstellar spaces and came from them just as our bodies came from the sea). And in fact there is no emptiness between the stars and the galaxies. The whole universe is really a single mass of matter, more or less rarefied or concentrated, and the whole cosmos is a single body.

The elements of meteorites that come from far-off stars (calcium, iron, copper, phosphorus) are the same as the elements of our planet, of our body, and the same as the elements of the interstellar spaces. So we are made of stars, or rather the cosmos is made of our own flesh. And when the Word was made flesh and dwelt among us, he could have said of all nature, as Adam said of Eve: "This now is flesh of my flesh and bone of my bones." In Christ's body, as in ours, the entire creation is incarnate.

In our bodies all living animals and all fossils are in communion with each other, along with the metals and the elements of the universe.

In our bodies all living animals and all fossils are in communion with each other, along with the metals and the elements of the universe. The sculptor working in stone is made of the same matter as the stone. The sculptor is like the consciousness of the stone, the stone turned artist, matter ensouled. And when we love God and are united with God, all creation and all its kingdoms, animal, vegetable and mineral, love God and are united with God too.

Nature is far more sacred to the Christian than it could have been to the pagan pantheist. We are more than pantheists because Christianity transcends any

All creation is a temple, says St. Gregory the Great. Every tree, stone, lizard, rabbit, meteor, comet, and star to us is holy.

kind of pantheism and the incarnation goes further than the wildest dreams of any particular philosopher.

Our bodies are sacred. They are *temples,* says St. Paul (and for the Jews nothing was more sacred than the Temple), and all nature shares in the holiness of our bodies. All creation is a temple, says St. Gregory the Great. Every tree, stone, lizard, rabbit, meteor, comet, and star to us is holy.

Singing in the Night

N ATURE CONSTANTLY communes with itself, feeding on itself and offering itself as food. Food is not prosaic; it is the communion of life. The Creator willed that in order to live we must eat other living beings because he wanted living beings to be in communion with one another. God did not want us to be independent of one another and self-sufficient. God wanted us to need to assimilate other living beings all the time so that through this assimilation we should remain in communion with the whole cosmos. The copepod eats the diatom, the herring eats the copepod, the squid eats the herring, the perch the squid, and when the perch dies and decays it in turn feeds the diatom or is eaten by humans, and human remains in turn feed the diatom — for life and death are all one, and life is constantly being reborn from itself. The fact that our flesh will have gone on to become the flesh of other beings needn't cause us to worry about the resurrection, because in this very process we are seeing the resurrection of the flesh already at work. With what body shall we rise? We shall rise with all bodies and all ages, or rather one single body will rise again, with many ages. In it we shall all be flesh of others and within one another as the foetus is in its mother. Only those who are not saved will be outside this body, and so the damnation of one person mutilates the body of Christ. And this is why St. Paul says that all creation, including plants and animals, is groaning in expectation of the resurrection of our body. And so only one body need rise to make it necessary that all bodies should rise. It is enough that Christ has risen — "the first born

Life and death are all one, and life is constantly being reborn from itself.

When we commune with Christ the whole cosmos communes with us.

from the dead" —to make it necessary for all creation to rise again.

Christ redeemed not only human nature but all nature. Bread and wine and water were also redeemed, and through Christ all matter has become holy and sacramental. Even the birds and the fishes of the sea share in the holiness of Christ and our holiness. Mother Nature became holy together with Mary the mother of Christ, for we are all in holy communion, from the lowliest invertebrates and mammals to the mother of God, and the humblest mammals also share in Mary's motherhood.

When we commune with Christ the whole cosmos communes with us. The Mayans believed that humanity was made of maize because they had an inkling of this communion and this mystical body. And Mayan sacrifices and all pagan eucharists were also a dark and imperfect sharing in this cosmic communion, this mystical body. As the Lord said to the Jews through the mouth of the prophet Malachi, God received sacrifices not only from Israel but also from all the pagan peoples on earth: "For from the rising of the sun to its setting my name is great among the nations, and in every place incense is offered to my name, and a pure offering; for my name is great among the nations, says the Lord of hosts" (Mal. 1:11).

Christ chose bread and wine for the Eucharist because this was the basic food and drink in the Mediterranean culture, which was the most universal at the time. And so this was the most universal food and drink. Wheat is the most widely grown cereal throughout the planet, but the bread and wine of the Eucharist represent all the fruits of the earth: maize, cocoa, coffee, tobacco, bananas, coconuts, pulque, and chicha.

And every fruit is like a synthesis of the whole cosmos. It is an assimilable chunk of cosmic matter, just as the bread and wine of the Mass are a synthesis and represent the whole cosmos. And they also represent our bodies, for our bodies are also fruits; we are these fruits assimilated and turned into bodies. Our flesh and blood are bread and wine. And when the bread and wine are changed into the body and blood of Christ, they symbolize our body and blood changed into the body and blood of Christ.

We all share in the same cosmic rhythm: the rotation

We all share in the same cosmic rhythm.

All natural laws, as the Book of Wisdom says, are like the rhythm of the strings of the harp.

of atoms and the circulation of our blood and the sap running through plants and the tides of the sea and the phases of the moon and the rotation of the stars in the galaxy and the rotation of the galaxies. It is all the same rhythm, all the same song, sung in chorus by the whole universe. For all natural laws, as the Book of Wisdom says, are like the rhythm of the strings of the harp. And the singing of monks and the liturgical cycle following the cycle of seedtime and harvest and the seasons of the year, and the cycle of life and death (and the life and death and resurrection of Christ) are part of this cosmic rhythm. It is a human sharing in the rhythm of the sea and the moon and animal breeding and the stars. And pagan liturgies also followed the harvest cycle and the seasons and joined in the cosmic rhythm that modern people in the cities have lost. For this rhythm is religion. As oysters depend on the rhythm of the sea for their breeding and other animals depend on the moon, human beings depend on ritual and the liturgical cycle. For as Ecclesiasticus says, it is religion that gives rhythm to human life. "Why does one day excel another, when all the light of every day in the year is of the sun?

By the knowledge of the Lord they were distinguished; and he altered seasons and feasts" (Ecclus. 33:7–9). And that is why life in cities like New York is so horribly monotonous.

That is why our religion is catholic, that is to say, universal, not just because it is the religion of all human beings but because it is the religion of the whole cosmos. It reaches from mollusks to the stars, it embraces all other rites and all that was true in all the ancient pagan religions, and it embraces more than religion — in the conventional sense of the word. It embraces the whole person (along with poetry, painting, folklore, dances, seedtime, and harvest festivals, the growth of plants and animals, and the love between men and women). Outside this religion there is no salvation.

The whole universe is a song, a choral chant, a festive song of the wedding feast ("A king made a wedding feast for his son"). We have not yet arrived at the feast, but we have been invited, and we see the light and hear the music from afar. "But at midnight there was a cry, 'Behold, the bridegroom! Come out to meet him'" (Matt. 25:6). And John the Baptist also proclaimed his arrival

The whole universe is a song, a choral chant, a festive song of the wedding feast.

The liturgy is the daily commemoration, here on earth and in time, of this wedding feast that has already begun in eternity.

and pointed him out: "He who has the bride is the bridegroom: the friend of the bridegroom who stands and hears him rejoices greatly at the bridegroom's voice" (John 3:29). The liturgy is the daily commemoration, here on earth and in time, of this wedding feast that has already begun in eternity. So for the Catholic Church all days are feast days and in the liturgy all the days are called *feria*, which means feast (the feast of Monday, the feast of Tuesday, and so on), and every day of the zodiacal and liturgical year is for us a symbol of the eternal feast that never ends. And our song, together with the chorus of stars and atoms is the same as the angels' chorus and the same as the song that may be sung by countless other spiritual races on countless other planets, a song to which the Book of Job seems to refer when it speaks of the morning stars singing together and the children of God shouting with joy. We are still in the darkness awaiting the bridegroom, but already we can see the light from far away and hear the singing in the night.